Last Rites

by Aram Saroyan

Last Rites
Genesis Angels
O My Generation and Other Poems
The Street
Poems
The Rest
Cloth
Words & Photographs
Pages
Aram Saroyan

B

SAROYAN, W.

Grateful acknowledgment is made for permission to reprint the following:

"After the Storm" by Boris Pasternak, from *In The Interlude: Poems 1945–1960.* Translated by Henry Kamen. Oxford University Press, England, 1962. Reprinted by permission of A. D. Peters & Co. Ltd.

Quotation from James Agee reprinted by permission of Grosset & Dunlap, Inc. from *Agee On Film,* Vol. 1, © 1958 by The James Agee Trust.

The article "Doctor Says Saroyan Has Cancer, Didn't Have Stroke" is used by permission of The Associated Press.

Library of Congress Cataloging in Publication Data

Saroyan, Aram.
    Last rites.

    1. Saroyan, William, 1908–   —Biography—Last years and death. 2. Authors, American—20th century—Biography. I. Title.
[PS3537.A826Z88]   818'.5209 [B]   82–448
ISBN 0–688–01262–0   AACR2

Printed in the United States of America

2 3 4 5 6 7 8 9 10

BOOK DESIGN BY PATTY LOWY

Last Rites

THE DEATH OF
WILLIAM SAROYAN

Aram Saroyan

C. 1

WILLIAM MORROW AND COMPANY, INC.
NEW YORK   1982

AUTHOR'S NOTE

This book comprises a journal that chronicles a highly charged passage in the writer's life. I make note of this here, at the beginning, in the hope of sparing the reader any avoidable feelings of being too rudely or abruptly jolted by the strongly emotional character of much that was written. On the other hand, and at the same time, it seems to me that whatever truth this book may contain consists in its fidelity to these very changes—moment to moment, as well as day by day—in the emotional quality of the experience it presents.

My father, William Saroyan, was, and remains today, a world-famous writer with a vivid public image. But as his son, I came to know a man very different from the one that the world at large seemed to insist he was. This gap between the public image and the reality I knew is very much a part of this journal.

Another part is the mystery and majesty, as well as the potential for healing, in the experience of dying: a passage we are only now beginning to recognize in all its wonder and power, as only a few years ago we began to recognize natural childbirth.

This is a book, then, about a famous man and his son —and about what might be called their last rites together. At a certain point during these events, it came to me poignantly that it was a book that my father himself would not be able to write. In the end, in the deepest and truest sense, I hope that I have written it the way he would want me to write it.

—ARAM SAROYAN
Bolinas, California

Special thanks to Sybil Christopher, Andrew Wylie, James Landis, Sally Furgeson, and Gailyn Saroyan.

AFTER THE STORM

The air is heavy with the passing storm.
The world revives and breathes in paradise.
Through all the clusters of its blossoming
The lilac drinks freshness and vivifies;

And life pervades all in the weather's change
As over roofs the gutters flood their rain,
But brighter still grows heaven's distant range,
Higher beyond the dark clouds its blue chain.

Transcendent power lies in the artist's hand
That cleanses all things from impurity
And from his color-bath newly transformed
Emerge the past, life, and reality.

Then memories of half a lifetime's age
Recede now with the passing of the storm:
This century outgrows its tutelage
To clear a way for all the years to come.

It is not some upheaval or uprising
Can lead us to the new life we desire—
But open truth and magnanimity
And the storm within a soul afire.

—BORIS PASTERNAK

My sister, Lucy, phoned yesterday evening to tell me she had received a phone call from my father's lawyer, Aram Kevorkian, and he had told her Pop is dying of cancer. He had, originally, prostate cancer, which apparently can be cured, but he didn't do anything about it, and it moved into his liver and now is in his bones.

I saw, clearly, right away, that the issues between us, before I knew this had happened to him, were now no longer significant.

He was told last September that he would probably not make it to 1981. He apparently has no interest in going into the hospital—and so far at least isn't experiencing any significant pain, although Lucy mentioned there is some pain at night.

He is seventy-two years old; he has had a good, strong, long life. Just the other night, I was reading a book of his which was published only five years ago, *Sons Come & Go, Mothers Hang In Forever,* and realizing how good it was, that he was right up at the top of his form, as Edward Hoagland had put it in a review in *The New York Times Book Review* that had pleased him very much at the time.

That the word of his illness is now, however fortuitously, filtering down to Lucy and me (and we are apparently the first to know other than his doctor and Aram Kevorkian) means to me simply that he wants us to know now, though he is probably troubled by misgivings as to how we feel about him—especially, most likely, me, since I've been out of touch with him now for going on four years.

And yet, strangely, I have felt perhaps less real distance this way than I would have otherwise. I have been able to love and respect him at a distance as I wasn't quite able to do before, seeing and writing to him. He is so shy and private a man in his actual life, as distinguished from his public life, that at a certain point it occurred to me that even his semiannual one- or two-hour visits with us and his grandchildren had, over the course of three years, grown to threaten seriously his threshold for intimacy.

And then, when I had an auto accident, fracturing my ankle in 1978, and he wrote me a silly and insulting letter, suggesting I had been at fault, perhaps on marijuana, etc., when the accident itself couldn't have been more clear-cut—I reached the crest of a hill to find a motorcycle coming at me in my lane at seventy miles an hour, about a car's length away when I first saw it—when I got the letter, I answered it immediately, and then decided not to mail it, because I didn't want to deal anymore with such draining, pointlessly undermining lack of basic credence on his part.

Not that there wasn't some shadow of substance to any doubt he, or for that matter anyone else in the world, might have about me—there always is. But when you are down, you don't want to hear about it.

This support is what I would like to give him now, if I am able to. He has done so very well with his life, and I am glad he is not encumbered with the degrading hospital procedures for cancer. I feel quite clearly that he is ready to die, and that he knows how to die, and that Lucy and I must simply do whatever we can for him to make his dying comfortable.

It is a natural thing, in his case. He has done what he was supposed to do, and, at the same time, this final episode of his life will very likely be an important one for me to go through with him, one from which I will learn.

Last night after receiving the call, I stood in the living room talking to Gailyn and the kids about the situation, going at it objectively, if perhaps somewhat numbly, when Gailyn said that our older daughter, Strawberry, who is ten, was upset.

"Are you sad, honey?" I said.

"Well . . ." she said, and then turned away on the couch in tears.

That did it, and I scarcely know whether it was my father or my daughter who really moved me, but my eyes were filled with tears and I went to hug her.

"Do you remember him?" I asked her.

"Of course," she said.

The simplicity of her grief was a great relief to me. It is a simple thing, after all, for someone to be dying, and it brings back the most important things you have shared together, the moments of truest intimacy, perhaps because death itself is so intimate. The rest becomes irrelevant.

Lucy called yesterday with the news that Pop's doctor in Fresno, Dr. Jibelian, had phoned her, after giving her a rundown on Pop's condition the day before, to say that in examining him again yesterday, he saw that his condition had worsened, and he no longer expected him to live beyond another two months—and that it could even be a matter of weeks. He had first told her he could go on for a year or more—or less.

He said Pop now has a large tumor in his liver which is excreting poisons.

I had suspected as much. I'd said to Lucy yesterday that if he was now, however circuitously, letting people know of his illness, after holding off for so long, it probably meant that he himself knew he was close to the end.

Lucy will drive up to Fresno today from Beverly Hills to offer whatever help she can. Tomorrow, we will all drive up as a family, check into a motel, and I will drive over with Armenak, our four-year-old son, whom he has seen least of all the kids, and spend a little time with him. We'll see if he wants to see Gailyn and Strawberry and Cream—or whether this would tax his energy too severely.

Gailyn said she wanted to be there with the whole family just in case he wanted to see us all. It's also possible that it will be easier for him to do this now than it will be later.

*   *   *

Lucy called this afternoon, after arriving in Fresno and going to my father's house.

"Forget it, Ar," she said.

And then I could hear her tears. She had driven up from L.A. with a basket of food and every good wish for him in her heart and he had abused her viciously and kicked her out of his house.

She was standing in a phone booth in the Fresno heat, crying and talking to me.

She had put on some perfume before going to his door because she had been sweating in the heat driving up, and he told her that her stink was killing him faster.

She had left her basket of food on his doorstep as she walked out of his house.

How well I know the black poisons of his soul that engulfed her today. How long I have known them, since the very beginning of my life, how well I understand them even, and how hard it is for me to forgive him even so.

Now he is dying, the only reason conceivable that I would reconsider seeing him, because he breathes a toxic paralyzing air that at any moment may replace the real air between us. He is a man who has lived for sixty-nine of his seventy-two years with these poisons, these big death-vibrations, and now he is dying and they are still there —perhaps even fiercer in his final days.

But this is William Saroyan, I can hear people saying, the author of *The Human Comedy* and *The Time of Your Life,* the wonderful crazy Armenian poet, the lover of life and all people everywhere.

And I am Aram Saroyan, his thirty-seven-year-old son, and somehow the old numb feeling had been growing in me all afternoon, as we approached our own visit with him, even before Lucy's call, which only heightened the feeling: the numbing that one knows when there is no way in the world to reverse this tide of hate and brutal, hysterical anger from him—and it has nothing whatsoever to do with you.

He wanted me to die, he wanted me to be a disgrace and a failure, to be a blot on his good name—the hopeless fuck-up son of a great man. Someone who kills innocent people driving down the wrong side of the highway. Someone who shoots heroin and dies of an overdose because he can't face the world. Somebody who drives off a cliff and kills himself the way his mother's brother, his Uncle Aram's son Chesley, killed himself after he failed to become a writer. He wanted me to be a failure like Chesley, so he could stand at my funeral, the big, wonderful, disappointed father.

My father never liked me or my sister, and he never liked our mother either, after an initial infatuation, and in fact, he never liked anyone at all after an hour or two, no, no one except a stooge, someone he could depend on to be a lackey, a nitwit he could make fun of behind his back, someone he could control completely by whatever means he could make work—fear, intimidation, or, because he was a famous and admired man, blind worshipfulness.

And he wanted me and Lucy and my mother to die. And he didn't kill us.

He didn't murder us except in a book called *The Laughing Matter* where it was OK to have my mother kill herself, where he couldn't be sent to the penitentiary for her death. He didn't kill us, but he initiated and carried out a long, in Lucy's and my case a lifelong, psychological war against us, so that we went numb with disbelief and sorrow and deep, deep, murderous anger.

A human life, after all, is a small thing in comparison

with the depths of such an anger. An anger such as my father's, which he releases at us, and only us, and an anger such as my own and such as my sister's and such as my mother's, which we do not release. For perhaps we are not so clever as my father is—perhaps we might lose control and murder literally, physically, rather than spiritually and psychologically, as he murdered Lucy today.

He is, indeed, a terribly clever man, as clever as the cleverest lawyer he detests. A terribly clever man, because, after all, a bully must be clever not to be exposed as a coward. He must choose his fights carefully not to be exposed by one who is evenly matched and willing to fight back. And my father was extremely clever and extremely careful.

He chose his wife, and his son, and his daughter.

I have a problem. I have a very hard problem that I don't seem to know how to handle, and over the years I have tried various approaches to it, and yet it seems to remain a problem no matter how I approach it; and the problem is how do I tell the real truth, how do I get it said in such a way that it is not a fraction of what it really is—but the whole insane immensity of itself; the rather preposterously negative immensity of it? Because there is a truth in it that is the truth at the very bottom of my life.

There is not will enough for suicide in that place. There is only the slow passing of time, of day minutes and night minutes, of the soul poised in its earthly container, simply there like a child at a window, looking out at nothing.

Like a child looking out at nothing—which is, I suppose, the deep lesson in what my father is, the deepest lesson in all his language written and spoken, to me and to others, in his books and not in them, the power in them as well as the pitiful fury of his life.

I am speaking of a man whose own father died before he was three years old. He was a year and a half younger at the time than my own son, Armenak, named after my father's father, is now.

His father died of a ruptured appendix, an appendix which burst after he drank a glass of water his wife Takoohi brought to him, knowing he should not drink water, knowing it might kill him, but unable, apparently, to refuse his pleading—so that his mother, in a certain sense, killed his father.

Armenak was a handsome man with a big old-country mustache and the large, startled eyes of a deer. He had come to America, an ordained Christian minister from Armenia, with so sure a command of English that he soon established a warm friendship with the Reverend William Stonehill of New York, after whom he eventually named my father, the only one of his four children to be conceived and born in America.

For he quickly landed his own parish, heading the Armenian Orthodox Church in Paterson, New Jersey; and, having found this work, he sent at once for his wife and children.

But Takoohi didn't take to Paterson. She wanted to move to Fresno where many other Armenians from their town, Bitlis, now lived, and they were written to by people already living there that Armenak would have his own parish.

And so, eventually, the family moved out to Fresno, where my father was born on August 31, 1908.

But there was no parish—or at least nothing of the size that would make it possible for Armenak to make his living through it.

Here was a man of delicate, other-worldly sensibility —a man already in his mid-thirties, ill equipped to forget his own deepest promptings and strike out on a new course of action, a man already biologically too old for that, perhaps, a man just settling into the contours of his own identity, after years of studies and rehearsals. But a man with a wife and four children, a man for whom a new course of action was a vital necessity.

Armenak Saroyan became a chicken farmer.

And then one afternoon, in the heat of a Campbell summer, he was brought into the house, off his feet, by two farmhands, and laid down on a sofa from which he never rose.

My father was the youngest of the children who were taken by their mother, Takoohi, to the Fred Finch Orphanage in Oakland, where they would live for the next five years of their lives. Henry, my father's brother, the youngest but for him, was six. Zabelle, his younger sister, was nine, and Cosette was twelve.

It was my father, alone, who was still in the middle of those first six years in which, according to Freud, the human organism experiences its deepest psychological impressions. If these years are without serious trauma, perhaps the organism can withstand a great deal without serious psychological consequences. But my father was at the age when a serious shock could have an impact on his nervous system which might remain for a lifetime.

And so it has. And what was the impression?

The loss of his father—sudden, and irrevocable.

And then, soon afterward, at the orphanage, just as suddenly, the loss of his mother—though, now working as a domestic, she would return for periodic visits, and, in five years' time, helped by Uncle Aram, her brother, she would take him and his brother and sisters to their own little home in Fresno.

*   *   *

But by then, he was eight years old—the impression had been made, strong and clear and irrevocable. He had it inside him—like a mirror with a slight warp in it which gives everything back slightly changed in reflection. That warp in my father was *loss,* pure and simple.

Yet, by some cosmic grace, some unaccountable strain of pure luck, my father emerged intact. Sound of body but, more than that, and far less likely, with a strong mind and a strong spirit, full of humor and daring and song.

He might have, with less cause for explanation, emerged an eight-year-old human cipher, understandably devastated by his misfortunes. Instead he emerged, by some infinitely complicated spiritual and psychological alchemy, an eight-year-old nascent genius.

Selling newspapers now in Fresno to help out at home. Sneaking into the movie house across the street from his corner to see special parts of special Charlie Chaplin movies. Growing up now in a growing California town, learning about everything under the sun.

This was the arena of his fondest writing; it was now that his life claimed its deepest resources in the whole spectacle of a small town's life: business and pleasure, school and sport, the comic and the sorrowful.

He dropped out of school in the eighth grade—mostly from boredom. But by twenty, strong and handsome and determined to become a writer, he was the youngest manager of a Postal Telegraph office in the country, after having started there as a messenger after school.

By now the whole family had moved to a house on Carl Street in San Francisco, where his sisters and his brother also had jobs. And then one day he quit his job at the Postal Telegraph office because he *had* to be a writer—it was now or never. And at twenty-six, after his exasperated Uncle Aram tried to throw him out of his own house for being a bum, until stopped by his mother's protests—at twenty-six my father sold his first story, "The Daring Young Man on the Flying Trapeze," to *Story Magazine.* And when it was printed he became an overnight sensation.

Where is the loss? Where is the problem?

Nowhere. Or nowhere yet. Or nowhere anybody would know it yet—because my father was a good writer, at his best a wonderful, true writer, and he was even, at this stage, making his loss work for him, making it come out into his sentences as a special, unexpected, poetic dimension, permitting it to be a kind of shadow within the sunlit pages of his youth, giving a kind of depth of field to his gaiety. But this was youth, when the energy is still building the blossom, before it will open fully to the light of day, and be known in its entirety.

Youth, in fact, was his truest time, the time he remains known for though he has lived a full lifetime. Nothing he has done since has ever matched his achievement here.

It was only after this, when the blood began to slow, that the loss began to show itself fully. It was only when he began to need the support of something other than his own no longer burgeoning vitality. It was, at thirty-five, the age his father Armenak had died, all at once, the war and . . .

The war hurt him because during the Depression he had been a singer, he had sung people right through the blues. He knew how to handle the Depression, he had been handling it since he was three years old. But when the mood changed, when everybody got ready to fight to kill, he felt at a sudden loss.

He knew the deepest death of all inside him, every day of his life, and yet he kept it at a safe, employable, ready-at-hand, but casual distance. He handled it swiftly, with an aesthetic aptness of touch, but without getting dangerously intimate.

Because he knew deep in himself how dangerous the loss was. Emptiness; nothing—where before he had had a father and a mother. He knew *exactly* how dangerous it was. It was death itself, the stinking, gaping, poison itself, down there—the warp in his own mirror. Death, and . . .

Love?

Because, quite suddenly, at thirty-five, he ran into a young woman, a girl really, just seventeen years old, just the sight of whom . . . turned the mirror true again, you could almost say.

Suddenly, he saw something out there that didn't simply touch him or make him laugh; he suddenly saw something so clear and beautiful that it stopped his mind, almost. Made it a true mirror again, a pure mirror—and, ow! There is where he could suddenly feel it again for real.

Feel the time when he was almost three—father gone, mother gone. The clear mirror of the unruffled little lake of his nervous system, holding all things in its child's embrace, suddenly back again—before it turned to glass, still a mirror, but glass, no longer water, and with a warp in it.

When he saw my mother he saw her so clearly—as only love sees—and instead of the glass, it was water again, the lake before it froze.

He was in love.

But he was also dying, wasn't he? The way he had been

dying as a child when he, quite literally, "froze his losses." And the mirror became glass, hard instead of soft, and perhaps even *sharper* because of it, less likely to get ruffled, but with a warp in it.

My mother and my father got married and divorced twice each by the time I was eight years old.

He was in a kind of sustained agony—shouting at his young bride, who was an innocent girl, really, who had fallen for a handsome and famous writer, and found herself in a frightening drama over which she could exert scarcely any control.

She remarried him, she told me, because when he called her to ask her, after she refused him, he asked to speak to me, and when I put down the phone, I started crying.

I was six years old and missed my father.

"Tell Aram," he told Lucy today when he found out that I knew he was dying, "not to come, not to write, and not to phone. Tell him he'll kill me if he does."

But he is very literally *dying* now, whether I arrive or not. He is speaking here, I think, not so much of dying as of feeling a strong emotion, which a visit from me and my wife and family might trigger in him, a terror far greater to him, I believe, than dying itself is.

He screamed at his thirty-five-year-old daughter today, whom he hasn't seen in a decade, as if he were almost three again and throwing the tantrum he wasn't allowed to throw at the time. But he is a seventy-two-year-old man now who is dying of cancer, whose daughter came up to help him.

Why is he screaming at her? Saying things I will not repeat here because they are so ugly and pointless and false?

Because he doesn't want to have to say thank you to Lucy, or to me—not that either of us would want it of him.

Dying now, with cancer through almost his entire body, he is still utterly in confusion and the deepest psychological pain when he registers even an inkling of his own emotional need.

He cannot afford emotional needs. He hasn't been able to afford them since he was almost three years old.

He cannot afford to be grateful—that, in itself, would be a recognition of emotional need.

This is, in fact, I believe, the same reason he turned down the Pulitzer Prize. He preferred not to feel gratitude.

He is an old man in a tract house in Fresno, dying of cancer. When his daughter came to offer her care, he was not able to accept it, and he told her this.

"You've come here to exploit my death."

And he added: "You want to be with a great writer."

Not her father—a great writer. It is as if fame were the only love he could accept in his life without falling into an emotional panic.

It's like a fairy tale.

The lake inside the child turns to glass, a mirror, and the artist is made, and the artist becomes world-famous, but he remains rigid inside, a glass mirror, frozen rather than fluid.

And then he falls in love, and the glass turns back into water. Love's element unfreezes his very character structure, the means, perhaps, by which he has survived at all in the first place—and, somehow, also the means by which he has become a famous artist, adored by people all over the world, but not yet loved by and not yet loving one person truly.

Love touches him inside and the mirror turns to a lake again, and he screams in pain.

He hates his wife *because* he loves her.

And then he hates his son and his daughter too.

Because the lake is filled with Death, the terrible death of his father, and the seeming death of his mother which he endured in being consigned to the orphanage at three.

He hates his wife *because* he loves her, and his wife who

is still a child, really, doesn't know what she has done wrong, and wonders if there isn't in fact something very wrong with her for what she has done, for what she seems always to do to this man.

But no matter what she does, no matter how much she grows, no matter how deeply she tries, she will never succeed, because he will hate her exactly as and when and *because* he loves her.

Because love turns the mirror, the glass, back into the lake, the water.

And there is pain, there is death itself, in the water. As if his dead father's body itself is in the water.

And then it becomes complicated, even more complicated and unfortunate than it already is.

Because he is famous.

He is not just a man with a very complicated, and in a specific way, a very destructive character structure—he is also a world-famous writer whom people love for the sweetness of his books.

He is, in fact, the most famous man of his nation who has ever lived. He is the most famous Armenian of all time.

And the Armenians, of course, are all very proud of him, they all love Saroyan, understandably, and look to him as a national treasure. He has given them an international fame and recognition at a time in which their own nation has been deprived of its independence, at a time in which they have been subject to genocide, both physically and spiritually.

And Saroyan is all that many people know of Armenia and Armenians. And the Armenians, understandably, love and adore Saroyan as their poet, their spokesman, their champion in a world that has been full of terror and depravity—a murderous world not unlike the world in

Saroyan himself when he unfreezes, if only for a moment, and feels it.

Which is the same moment when, as he did yesterday, he screams.

When this happens, when he feels the pain, when he knows the terror in himself, that is also the moment that he dismisses his reality, the pain he feels but does not understand, will not dare look at lest it destroy him completely, kill him outright—it is like a reflex now, so practiced and engrained has the movement of his psyche become over the years.

It is at just this moment of complete terror and pain and madness that he remembers he is a famous writer.

"You're here to be with a great writer," he told Lucy yesterday.

He is not dying now figuratively. It is not spiritually, or emotionally, or psychologically that he is threatened now—he is quite literally *dying* now, physically.

And yet the mechanism for relief remains unchanged.

In the early days, after a blowup with my mother, he would run to the Armenians, who embraced him and sympathized with him and all but gave him the crown and the scepter because it would be impossible, after all, that this wonderful man, this poet of people and light and laughter and fruit and bread and water, this profound and beautiful soul was not being taken advantage of viciously by this girl, who was herself in fact not even an Armenian, but Jewish.

A gold digger, perhaps.

And my father would be comforted, and calmed, and restored to his psychic balance, reintegrated by the healing presence of the people who loved him but whom he loved less specifically and dangerously than he loved my mother.

And after a while, perhaps, he fell in love with something a little less painful than another person—a little less dangerous, and if unpredictable in the larger world, at least steadfast among the Armenians. My father, I think, a little later on in his life, after it was clear to him that he couldn't afford any more demanding entanglement, fell in love with Fame itself.

The summer I was fifteen years old, in 1959, Lucy and I stayed with him in Paris while he wrote a book called *Not Dying*. One afternoon, alone in the house, I came across the following note, written in his hand on a piece of typing paper: "The only person I have ever really loved is Saroyan, and all that I really love now is the little of Saroyan still left in me."

I called Lucy in Beverly Hills yesterday afternoon after speaking with my father's doctor, the Armenian Dr. Jibelian, in Fresno, and letting him know, so that he could pass it along to Pop, that his grandchildren—Strawberry, Cream, and Armenak—would like to see him, and if he would like to see them, we would be happy to make the trip to Fresno and drop them off with him for a short visit—or have a third party, perhaps Dr. Jibelian himself, take them to him.

This offer was made as a last formality, more or less, through Dr. Jibelian, who urged Lucy to come to see her father and hence is himself aware—since Lucy phoned his office after Pop had kicked her out of his house—that we are not an ordinary family.

Lucy told me that when she first arrived at the house on West Griffith Way in Fresno, there was a man gardening in front. Since Lucy had never been to the house before, she asked the man if he knew who lived inside.

"Oh, yes," he said. "Mr. Saroyan."

She then told him who she was, and he introduced himself as a distant relative, Ruben Saroyan. He said he was delighted to meet her because her father spoke of her so often and so fondly.

When she got to the door and knocked, my father yelled from inside, "Who is it?"

Lucy said, "It's me, Pop."

Pop yelled back, "Lucy? What are *you* doing here?"

And then he opened the door. She said he looked, under the circumstances, "fine."

"Well," Lucy said when she saw him, "I'm here for *you,* Pop."

"That's horseshit," he answered. Even normally, his voice is very loud; he has been deaf in one ear since early childhood. "Come off the horseshit."

Lucy said the gardener, hearing this, retreated to a corner of the front yard.

In effect, he had already started yelling at her when she stepped into the house and sat down for a moment, putting down her basket. She was, I can imagine, overwhelmed by his viciousness, but she had come a long way and for all she knew this was the last she would ever see of him.

He slandered her viciously—playing on her own insecurities, her not being married, or famous, or rich.

"Does Aram know?" he asked.

"Yes, he does."

"Oh *great,*" my father yelled. "Just *great.*"

He told her that he could kill Aram Kevorkian for phoning her. That if he had the physical strength in him he would kill him.

Aram Kevorkian ordinarily lives in Paris, where he does legal work for my father, who maintains an apartment there. Apparently he had to spend some time in Fresno for reasons of his own, and while there spent a day with my father—"an immortal day," Pop wrote in a book he inscribed for him—and during the course of that day, driving around Fresno visiting relatives and vineyards, Pop told the lawyer, an amiable pear-shaped man as I remember him from Paris fifteen years ago, that he had cancer. Kevorkian was apparently the first person outside

of Dr. Jibelian to know. The lawyer then suggested that
Lucy and I be informed.

"Oh no—they hate me," Pop had said.

But then he had softened and told Kevorkian that Lucy
might spend an hour or two a day with him if she were
there. I can imagine Lucy packing her bags when she
heard that. Over the past five years, she has been writing
my father periodic fond, conciliatory letters to which he
has never responded at all. Now, suddenly, she had
something in the nature of a specific summons from him
to come up to Fresno and be with him.

After hearing that I, also, knew, Pop yelled at Lucy: "Is
he a *writer*? I mean is he supposed to be a writer?"

"Yes, he is, Pop," Lucy said.

"That's just great," he said sarcastically.

"And he's also," Lucy told me she added with feeling,
"a wonderful father."

"Well, yes," Lucy imitated Pop saying curtly. "That's
one thing he has over you."

I know the devastation she felt in those few minutes
that she was there. I can imagine her in the dark living
room crowded with books and boxes and papers, with
the sun blazing hot at the windows, sitting there, my little
hundred-pound sister, getting punched around by my
dying father.

"Well . . ." she said, now resigned to defeat, but
perhaps hoping for some last shred of dignity. "I brought
some food . . ."

"What have you got in that basket?" my father asked
her gruffly.

"Well," Lucy answered, "I brought some chicken . . ."

"All right, now," he said. "You take your chicken and
your pot, and you get out of here."

Lucy told me over the phone that she couldn't tell if

he meant the pot chicken is sometimes cooked in, or marijuana.

When she got outside, just a few minutes after arriving, dropping the basket of food inside his house just before walking out the door, she found that the gardener, who could not have helped but hear his screaming, had already left.

After leaving the house, Lucy found that she was now in a panic, an irrational panic, to get to a phone and stop me from coming down. There was, in fact, no imminent danger of this, since, as I've said, we had planned beforehand that I would be leaving the next day. We had discussed both of us going to his house together, which I had wanted to do, along with Armenak, but Lucy had insisted, and I had finally agreed, that it would be better for her to arrive first and establish her presence with him, since she planned to stay on after we left.

She drove, crying, in her car in the Fresno sun and heat, nearly running into a man on a bicycle.

Once on the phone with me, as she told me what had happened, she repeated over and over again to me like a refrain: "Don't come down here, Ar. Don't come, Ar. Don't. Don't come down here."

I knew that she was speaking both literally and figuratively, from the pit of self-annihilation into which he had plunged her. But it was Lucy herself I was hearing, my sister, who loves me and my family, and who had just done one of the bravest deeds I can imagine anybody ever doing, and gotten brutalized viciously for doing it.

Yesterday, back in Beverly Hills, when she picked up the phone and said "Hello," I heard the word spoken by someone else entirely. I heard the two syllables break in half as she said the word with hardly the force to issue it. In the twenty-four hours since we had last spoken, Lucy had let it sink in fully.

She hardly wanted to talk.

I sense that my father will try to arrange his will for the least possible benefit to Lucy and me, his two legitimate heirs, and I wanted to tell her, having discussed this with Gailyn now, that I am ready to contest any inequities in it—for our own sake, and our children's and his grand-children's sake, and for Lucy's sake.

Lucy didn't want to hear about it. She sounded as if she had just woken up—I asked her if she had, and she said no, she had been up since nine, but she had just fallen asleep and been in the middle of a nap. She sounded as if she had taken a down.

She made me feel guilty about thinking about the will, as if it were an avaricious and outright evil thing to think about when my father is dying. Perhaps it is—but under the circumstances, I don't think so.

He didn't want to see us before, not really, because we reminded him of our mother, and she reminded him of the death inside him all his life.

Now, though, a paradoxical change has occurred. When he heard Lucy's voice on the other side of the door, he must have known instantly that she knew he was dying—why else would she come?

Why else would *I* ever come?

That summer I was fifteen in Paris, I had wanted to leave almost immediately after Lucy and I had arrived. I was bored: Pop was writing, there was nothing to do, I couldn't speak French. But Lucy wouldn't let me leave. She loved him, always, more than I did.

Yesterday I had a moment, just the sheerest flicker of a realization that he was going—my father would, one day not too far from now, be gone, and I had a quick interior shudder.

A shudder for the change to come in my own interior architecture: as if a huge wall were to be suddenly removed and sunlight to flood in where for years what has grown has been an issue of darkness.

I had, to speak of, no real father.

I knew my mother intimately. This past year I had a dream in which I visited her, and then her friend upstairs, Gloria Vanderbilt, in an identical apartment. There was a difference between their apartments that was impossible not to notice, and I commented to Gloria on it.

"Well, you see," Gloria explained, "your mother's furniture all points *in* to the room, whereas all of mine is directed outward toward the windows, the outside."

My mother, a Virgo like my father, has an entrenched inner life—and even now, writing of it, I am impatient of exploring it, I feel a heat suddenly in the pit of my stomach. The whole effort of these last years for me—the whole effort of my adult life, perhaps, but consciously now, for survival itself as a man, as an artist, as a husband and a father—is to turn my own furniture *out* toward the windows, the light, the world.

Dr. Jibelian called yesterday before noon to let me know he had spoken with Pop and that he didn't want the kids to visit, although the doctor said he tried to convince him that it would be good for him to see them, but that he would like to have some snapshots of the kids and ourselves, too, and that he appreciated the thoughtfulness of our gesture, and that he loved us. Did he say this last for the doctor or ourselves, I wondered.

Rather than try to remove photographs, I simply sent him our latest scrapbook. When I insisted on knowing what Pop's condition was, and how long he had to go, the doctor said "a month, maybe two." (He had asked me to send the pictures special delivery, which I did.) He said that it was a day-by-day thing now, and could change for the worse at any time—if the cancer, for instance, which has moved from his prostate to his liver and into his bones, moved now to his brain, which I assume would induce a coma. The doctor assured me he would phone if there were any significant change.

I will phone him on Monday to suggest the possibility of Pop's receiving help from Hospice, which has an office in Fresno, and might provide home visits there. My sense is that Pop will refuse this, but there is at least some possibility that he won't, since the care could be for as small an amount of time as he wished, and it would be less personal than any provided by a family member or by anyone with whom he is at all intimate, which he seems to want to avoid.

Last night I lay in bed, remembering scenes with Pop, and telling Gailyn of them. The scenes came at random, with no apparent point of emphasis. The imminence of his death has seemingly thrust me into the field of his whole lifetime, as I know it, either personally or more indirectly. The whole terrain is about to be closed, to become finite, and I find myself grappling to discover its basic order. I must do this less for his sake than for my own. If I can understand him, and myself in relation to him, I can spare myself the anger and resentment that is so much a part of what is between us.

The earliest memory last night was of visiting the middle-aged son of a movie mogul at his mansion somewhere, I believe, in a still-wooded area of Beverly Hills, in the early fifties after my mother and father had remarried. This marriage was almost over before it began, but it is the one period in my childhood in which I actually remember my father living in the house with us.

The mogul's son was a friend of my father's of an order that over the years he has seemed most to prefer—that is, he was a man to whom my father felt fundamentally superior. As I remember it, more than thirty years ago now—I couldn't have been more than seven at the time —my father had explained to me that this man was living in the shadow of his famous and powerful father, that he was a nice boy—I don't know if he actually used this word, but the implication was certainly there—who was now in fact a middle-aged man, who simply would never achieve anything, was in fact a complete ineffectual, an affable, easygoing rich boy. A total loss.

But my father spent time with him, liked him, and, at least on this one occasion, visited him, and I don't remember his visiting anybody else at that time.

My father's friend, an amiable balding man of medium build, had two Irish setters, the most beautiful and gently friendly dogs I had ever seen, and I remember those great dogs as we stood in front of his house, which crested a slight rise on his property. Lucy was also with us. We stood talking for a moment, playing with the dogs, and then we went inside the house.

The real memory occurs inside the house—it is something I have seen in my mind's eye at least once or twice a year ever since. Our host, my father, Lucy and

I all step into a small studylike room, wood-paneled, and there is a dart board against the far wall. There is immediate interest in the dart board (not least my own interest) and I see my father take the three darts and, now standing on the other side of the room, fire them swiftly into the target—one two three—a bull's-eye! then one right next to it! and then one right next to that! And the three darts, right next to each other, were in a perfectly straight line.

I looked on it as a minor miracle. I had never seen my father play darts before, and to this day I have never seen him play them again. He did tell me years later that one of the major dream motifs of his life was of a target, and of trying to make a bull's-eye.

"Hey, good shots, Bill," said my father's friend mildly with a smile. I think I was too amazed to say anything at all.

How did he make those three flawless shots? Last night I said to Gailyn what I have always believed but never uttered to anyone else before, scarcely letting my own inner ear hear it—that he made the shots because the movie mogul's son, to whom he felt superior, was there, and so he was both very relaxed and extra confident, and this gave him the power, perhaps the outright magic, to do what he did.

After speaking with the doctor yesterday, I phoned Lucy when I found that I no longer had Pop's Fresno address, and that I no longer even remembered it, at least not the exact numbers I needed to send him the photo album. She was rallying.

"I've got diarrhea, Ar. All the poisons are coming out of me."

"Great, Lu," I said, genuinely happy to hear her coming back to life.

I told her of the doctor's latest assessment of Pop's condition, and the time left.

And then I found myself saying something Gailyn and I had discussed but which I wasn't sure I should speak of to Lucy, being uncertain of her response.

"You know, I wasn't sure that after your visit, Lu, he wouldn't have a remission."

I felt as if I were raising a possibly sticky issue. I wasn't sure she wouldn't feel I was completely out of line—if not with her, then in my attitude toward Pop, toward cancer, toward death itself.

"So did I, Ar!" she said immediately and brightly. "I thought that what he got out on me should be worth six months or so."

So she had felt it just as we had. It was a relief to say it, and to hear her concur. If the facts contradict the feeling, in this instance, for me at least it remains a psychological truth, and another point of entry into the mystery of my father's life.

When I received the letter he wrote to me after the car accident—a letter that was poisonous when I was in the midst of trying to heal—I immediately sat down at my typewriter and answered it point by point. (No, I wasn't on pot, etc.) But I never mailed it. I wanted, suddenly, to break the circuit.

I sensed, clearly, that I was being emotionally blackmailed. I knew by now that I was, so long as I remained in any contact with my father whatsoever, to be the subject of periodic—entirely unpredictable, but nevertheless predictably periodic—attacks of psychological violence.

I hadn't, in any case, been in touch with him for half a year before the accident occurred, and he hadn't been informed of it for a full three weeks after it happened.

Knowing themselves, neither his brother nor his sister would voluntarily tell him, reckoning, I don't doubt, the likelihood of the kind of response he made. Finally, receiving sympathetic phone calls from both my aunt and my uncle, I couldn't help asking Cosette one afternoon whether my father knew, and when she said no I asked her to tell him, and a few days later received the letter.

My previous contact with him, six months earlier, had been a telephone call, during which he exploded as he exploded in person with Lucy on Wednesday. I don't believe my father would ever say to my face the things he has said to me over the telephone—he has been vicious to me, in fact, primarily on the telephone, after the age of thirteen or so. Whereas with Lucy, a woman and a small one at that, he has been more careless of the specific medium of communication.

So far as I know, he has never had a fistfight in his life, and is a confirmed physical coward. During his second divorce proceedings with my mother, sitting with the son of the movie mogul at the premiere of John Huston's movie *The Red Badge of Courage,* he talked to his friend so continually as the movie was shown that it finally prompted James Mason, who sat several rows in back of my father and his friend, and who had called for quiet several times, to get up out of his seat and go to my father and slap him, and again demand quiet. Only after he had done this did he recognize my father in the darkness of the movie theater.

"Oh, Bill—it's you. Well, damn it, be quiet."

This incident became a news item. My father apparently made no response whatsoever, either at the time or later to the press, except that he remained quiet for the rest of the film.

I do not write this with any particular sense of either

moral or physical superiority—I was a physical coward at fifteen at boarding school. Later, I had several fights and backed out of several others. I don't consider myself a fighter, and today I would incline to side with a nonviolent way of dealing with even those problems that sometimes seem to warrant violence.

This may simply be a way of my saying that I am a physical coward, but I choose to believe that having explored violence a few times at first hand, and trying on the attitude of the fighter myself for a while, I eventually came to regard it personally as a poor fit. I have found, in any case, that fighting means different things to different men. If one is raised with it, it can assume almost the character of sport, or at least something far less serious and threatening than it is for a young man, as I was, confronting his own fear both of his opponents and at the same time of the violence he feels within himself and is fearful of releasing.

My father's particular combination of violence and cowardice probably contributed directly to these fears of my own as a child. I remember once in the fifth grade—now living in a house in Pacific Palisades with my mother and sister, a house that was bought by my father, as part of the second divorce settlement, in my sister's and my name*—I remember astonishing both my classmates and

*My mother was never to prove herself at all as a fortune huntress. Having hired the famous Beverly Hills divorce lawyer, Jerry Geisler, to represent her in her second divorce from my father, she nevertheless refused both alimony and community property, and settled for $400 a month child support, out of which she paid the $175 monthly mortgage payment on the house. My father was always sporadic about making even these payments, and when my mother married Walter Matthau in 1959, at a time when Matthau was still seven years from stardom in Hollywood and already under the financial strain of his own previous marriage, with two children of his own to support, my

my teacher herself when, after I had provoked her by continuing to engage in some piece of mischief, she ordered me to leave the class and go to the principal's office.

In fact, what happened next astonished me, too. I found myself, a moment after being involved in lighthearted devilry, suddenly seized by a deep, literally quaking terror. I begged the teacher, an attractive woman named Mrs. Donovan, to please let me stay in class and promised her that I wouldn't disturb her again. But having apparently completely run out of patience, she refused to let me off.

Suddenly I was crying, and then, clasping my hands in front of me, I was on my knees in front of Mrs. Donovan and before the whole fifth-grade class, begging her to please, please not send me to the principal.

At this point, the young woman, no doubt astonished by this spectacle, started to laugh, and making light of it and at the same time dismissing me with still greater, but more casual and hence less menacing certainty, ordered me up off my knees, and out of the room to the principal's office.

In the retrospect provided only a few minutes later, I was grateful to her for not relenting. The principal, a creature who had suddenly come to assume the form of some unknown ghastly supernatural terror, someone who would literally exceed my wildest imagination, turned out to be an ordinary man, somewhat harassed by all the business of the afternoon, who not only didn't spank or whip me, or whatever magnificent atrocity might have matched my boundless terror, but hardly had time even to acknowledge my arrival and, moments later, my departure back to class.

---

father nevertheless stopped sending any further child support entirely. I was then fifteen, and Lucy thirteen.

All kids of my generation, of course, had heard stories of mean school principals, and in fact I had never before visited a principal's office, but even given these qualifications, my fear was extraordinary, and the only explanation that seems possible to me is that it was connected by some subterranean psychological equation with an unfathomed fear I felt in relation to my father.

For my father existed for me in two ways: both as a famous, admired man whom teachers and other adults were more or less continuously making note of in relation to me, and at the same time, as I had now gone through my parents' second divorce and was once again living alone with my mother and sister, as a deep, fathomless mystery—as, in fact, a kind of wall I could somehow never quite find the human contours of, as a kind of human wall.

Years later, in my young manhood now, and living in New York City where my mother had moved my sister and me after a few years in the Palisades, I remember taking a walk with my father through Manhattan as the evening approached and the light slowly diminished and the streetlights came on.

Walking through the darkening streets, I described to him a kind of myth that had taken shape in my mind some time before, and which I somehow felt it was important for him to hear and to know—and perhaps to suggest an ending for.

"What if you lived in a brownstone, Pop, you had an apartment, you know, in one of these brownstones, and you came home after work every night. And one night when you came home there was a man sitting on the stoop, somebody bigger than you are, and as you went up the steps, the man stood up in front of you and wouldn't let you pass, moved to the side when you

moved to the side, stayed in front of you no matter where
you moved to get past him—"

I think we were trying to find the house of a woman
my father had met the night before and was interested in
seeing again. He was looking for female companionship,
while I was, at this time, fairly certain that I was impotent.

"—and then eventually he'd let you pass. But the next
night when you came home again, he'd be there again,
and you'd have to go through the same thing all over
again. What would you do, Pop?"

What am I describing here? I ask myself, suddenly,
sitting up in this bed in our back bedroom in Bolinas,
where I have been writing since six this morning and it
is now lunchtime, twelve-thirty or so, rooted to this spot
to write this, to get it down where it can be seen for
whatever it is—what am I describing here, after all, but
the continuing skirmish of my very life itself, with my
father in front of me, the great writer, bigger than I, or
more famous, and no matter where I go, no matter how
I struggle to get past him, he is still there in front of me
—and yet, somehow, I finally get through, and go inside?

The man stays outside, and my life goes on inside—as
my mother's furniture is turned *in* to the room.

But the man is outside, in the world at large, whereas
my own deeper life, after my job in the daytime world,
goes on in my apartment at night. And there is a trouble-
some situation getting into that life—the man in front of
where I live—and so, both my leaving and returning
there is full of anxiety: the man will be there when I come
home; the man is in front of me when I want to go in.

And what of sexual impotence as well? Could I "go in"
in this way, past my father, who had somehow gotten
himself stuck outside—where did the man on my stoop
(my stoop—!) live, anyway, or was he only and forever
in front of me when I got home, forever and only an

obstacle to me, with no real life of his own? The man wasn't there when I went to my job in the morning—he wasn't there when I went to do something I had no real interest in doing—but only when I came home to whatever real life I could manage.

And, in fact, since his double marriage and double divorce to and from my mother, my father so far as I know has never had even a single serious affair. He goes to prostitutes, a form of sexuality that removes this normally, at least nominally, intimate experience to the impersonal level of a financial transaction. It is almost as if he insists that this one other dimension of his life that might in the normal course of events demand the same kind of human recognition he balked at with my mother, and with my sister and with me . . . it is as if he is determined to consign this final potentially intimate aspect of his life to the threat-free, almost impersonal domain of the call girl.

This is the man, after all, who turned down the Pulitzer Prize in 1940 for his play *The Time of Your Life* because he believed, he said, that "commerce had no business patronizing art." Love itself, however, proved to be something else again.

What was his advice regarding the man in the doorway in the myth?

First, as I remember, with a wry look that was familiar to me, he asked how it was that I would conceive of such a situation in the first place. How I answered this I no longer remember, and all I recall of his reply, which most likely involved other, earlier alternatives, were his final, impatient words, as if to dismiss the problem once and for all: "I don't know—hit him with a brick!"

The dawn breaks and I get up, make myself some breakfast, let out and feed the chickens, feed the cats. Just as I get back in bed the kids begin to wake up and discover their Easter baskets on the living-room table, where the Easter Bunny laid them out last night. Gailyn stirs beside me and tells me to make sure they only eat one candy now—no more until after lunch—which I call in to them. I hear Armenak exclaiming over something in the living room.

Last night, for just a moment before going to bed, I felt for my father, all alone dying of cancer in the night of his Fresno tract house. What was he doing? Was he walking around through his dark rooms, swearing at everything? Or was he set up in his bed with magazines and books all around and a big cup of hot cocoa, laughing at the radio talk shows?

Or neither?

But the feeling was just a stray fragment of emotion that didn't materialize. I knew he didn't want to see me, that he probably didn't want to see anybody, that he was as locked up in death now as he had been in life—perhaps, because of his physical weakness now, even more so. He can't break down and admit human frailty, and accept human succor. And now the cancer itself is breaking him down, week by week, day by day, perhaps even hour by hour—can he feel it working?—and carrying him, all by itself and with no significant human company in attendance, into the arms of death.

He will be released in death. I feel that clearly. He will be released out of his own willful, self-imposed exile in life. He will be one of the multitude in death, one of the numberless, as he couldn't be in life, except in momentary invention, except in momentary art.

What a supple style he had! What a marvel of ease, at its best something very close to breathing itself: *Inhale and Exhale* he called his second book of stories, and it was that natural a thing to him in his prime. A young man with a typewriter, a cup of coffee, and a pack of Chesterfields, singing in the Depression wilderness of America, singing with a distinctly American, an early improvising jazz style, and yet with just a touch of the old country music, the lyrical Armenian strain, that little shimmy in the line, a slight, imperceptible lilt that sent a pang right through the reader, that touched the blood itself.

For we were, *all of us,* from the old country, were we not? And America, at its best, was like some kind of vast and ultimately unknowable dreamland, all of us trading names and faces and homelands, recipes and memories in our sleep, the big waking dream of America itself.

Too many languages, too many histories, too many old-country relatives. And not enough time to think, and to remember; not enough time to, truly then, create. Who were we—with our umbrellas, and our garlic? With our rosaries, and our yarmulkes, and our Won Ton Soup? Who were we with our ancient alphabets and our Yellowstone National Park? Our automobiles and haircuts, our cigar-store Indian and our Brooklyn Bridge?

And then, suddenly, in the middle of the Depression in 1934, out at the far western end of the continent, sitting at the Barber College on Third Street in San Francisco, waiting for a fifteen-cent haircut during which his prodigious head of black hair would be used as a training ground for a future barber of America, probably another kid much like himself, there was young Saroyan, the Armenian American-born poet in prose, who saw everything in such a way that it made it beautiful again, and simple, and true—a style he had that used only the oldest and simplest and truest words, and that made those words into a song.

He was generous. He had enough hair on his head not to worry if the young barber, caught up for just a moment in the American spirit of adventure, sought a breakthrough in his own art form, the proper cutting of heads of hair. He didn't mind if the boy gave him a haircut that made his head look boxlike in its overemphasis on straight, clean, efficient lines. His hair, after all, would grow back, and the kid might be on the verge of a breakthrough that would eventually revolutionize his art.

This was America, after all. We were all willingly submitting ourselves to an experiment, and there was no sense getting extra fussy. After the haircut, for instance, there was a place he could go where for a nickel you could drink all the buttermilk you wanted. Five cents and you could have ten glasses. And they didn't mind if you did, in fact, *drink* ten glasses, because there were older, less rambunctious customers who would not require this kind of quantity, who would not take the challenge—"All You Can Drink for 5¢"—quite so literally to heart.

America was an economic experiment, but also, and more importantly, a spiritual one. As for the buttermilk itself, it was simply an excellent, sustaining food if you happened to have only a nickel to spend for nourishment that day.

Years later—I was spending the year at Trinity Pawling boarding school in upstate New York—when the American government was giving my father what he described as "a beating on my back taxes," when he owed them something in the neighborhood of $50,000 and it didn't seem likely that he would be able to make this amount of money in the discernible future, my father made the decision to move to Yugoslavia and once there to write and direct a movie, which might, in fact, be just the way to make so large a sum of money, and even more.

The Yugoslavian government was apparently delighted to have this distinguished writer as an émigré, and was also, apparently, more than willing to help with the making of the movie. On landing at the airport in Belgrade, he was met by a delegation of reporters, as well as officials from the government and the nationalized film industry. Everyone was excited about the film, a project that somehow was never to come to fruition. At the impromptu press conference my father gave at the airport, the first question was posed by a delegate of the film industry.

"Mr. Saroyan," the man asked earnestly. "How many horses will you require?"

"One," my father answered immediately. "Make it a white one."

This is the sort of moment that deeply delighted him.

When he took Lucy and me to Europe in the summer of 1957, during a visit to Venice, we happened to meet in a museum statuary another American, an enormous black man who introduced himself to us as Cess Pellam, and when my father in turn introduced himself and Lucy and me, he greeted us all warmly and with a fine sense of ceremony, though obviously unaware that my father was a famous writer.

The conversation was brief, standing among the ancient broken forms of the statuary under an overcast sky, as cats strolled the garden thoroughfares, along with one or two other visitors.

Cess Pellam was a very black man with a wonderfully loud and melodious voice. As we shook hands and said good-bye, my father said to this man, with the extra courtesy and goodwill he saved for such chance encounters, that it had been an honor to meet him.

"Well," answered Cess Pellam loudly, in his deep and easy bass vibrato, "it's been an honor for *both* of us!"

Somehow this wording struck me as funny, seeming to say both more and less than it seemed to mean, and for the rest of the summer I would periodically imitate Cess Pellam saying good-bye to my father this way, and it would never fail to break him up instantly and completely.

It was during this summer in fact that, employing a variety of voices and, in particular, a loud false voice which, in combination with a sort of catch-all pep talk ("Boys, the only way to do it is to do it! You've got to do it, boys, that's all. Would you do it? Please, boys. Do it!"), particularly delighted him—it was during this summer that having, I suppose, at last lucked on a sure-fire way to make positive contact with my father, I became something in the nature of an all day stand-up comedian.

In retrospect, that was perhaps the strangest summer of my life. After a few days at sea, on a ship called the *Vulcania* of the Italian Line, my father initiated what was to amount to a summer-long harangue to me (he consistently excluded Lucy for reasons of his own) on the subject of my mother.

He did this with such an urgency, and at the same time such a sure sense of how to maximize the drama of what he considered to be his own betrayal by her, that within

the first few days of his diatribe, my mother had changed
for me from a beautiful and loving young woman, one
with obvious shortcomings as a mother but with an overall sweetness of nature that made these seem unimpor-
tant, into a cunning, duplicitous, and, if the truth were
known, a fundamentally *evil* woman, who had ensnared
my father—who portrayed himself to me as a simple man
who only wished to found a family with a woman he
loved, and who he thought loved him—in a web of such
thorough and intricate deception that it could scarcely
have been better contrived by the Death Goddess Kali
herself.

Let me make it clear that I am speaking of myself at the
age of thirteen, at the very onset of my own sexuality,
having begun to masturbate with girlie magazines that
same year, as well as with remembered, glimpsed images
of my own mother, who was, as I say, a beautiful woman,
and scarcely thirty years old.

Let us say, entirely for the sake of argument, that everything he said about my mother (and I will get to the
substance of these attacks in a moment) but even more
important, and far more powerful in altering my own
image of who she was, everything he *implied* about her
nature in these angry and impassioned monologues to me
—let us say that absolutely everything he said and everything he implied about my mother was true.

Still, I cannot help but think, having a son of my own
now, that he would have been mistaken, utterly and indeed criminally mistaken, to have chosen such a time to
tell me these things. He gambled my own sexual adjustment as a man, at a time when it was at a most delicate
stage, in order to vent anger at my mother. Even if his
own anger were entirely justified, what he did would still
seem to me to be an act of deep psychological violence
by a father against his son.

*   *   *

What, exactly, had my mother done to him?

It is a strange catalog, each item of which, as he presented it to me, was less an independent proof of her dishonor than a part of a whole tissue of lies which, once glimpsed in its entirety, added up to something so monstrous and engulfing that it undermined the foundations of my father's most basic credence, his trust in my mother's actual reality itself, so that he in fact found it literally impossible to go on living with her.

I will take the three major deceptions one at a time, in no particular order of emphasis, since, as I say, it is not so much the parts, but the whole they make that is important:

1) She wasn't an heiress.

When they were first going together, she had been referred to in one of the New York columns as "heiress Carol Marcus." When they were married, this turned out not to be true. She had no money, to speak of, of her own.

2) She was Jewish, and she had told him that she wasn't. My father is probably less anti-Semitic than the average Armenian American of his generation, but among these Armenians, it was not uncommon to sit around after dinner and knock the Jews, another minority group in America and, like the Armenians, the victims of genocide in the twentieth century.

One night before they were married, my mother, who is Jewish—and who, when she met my father at seventeen, was just coming of age largely within the milieu in which she found herself, largely the world of Upper East Side debutantes—was with my father and a group of Armenians, and the conversation came around to the Jews, and all of a sudden there was a lot of knocking going on.

At one point, my mother was so upset by this talk that she noticeably winced. My father then wheeled around to her, and said: "What's the matter, kid— *you're* not Jewish, are you?"

Deeply in love with my father and frightened that he literally might not like her if he knew she was Jewish, she quickly, and almost by reflex, denied that she was.

"Oh no," she said.

3) She was illegitimate, and didn't tell him.

My mother's mother, whose maiden name was Rosheen Brophman, and whose family emigrated from a rural area near Kiev, Russia, is my father's age, having been born, like him, in 1908. She was strikingly beautiful as a young woman, just as beautiful as my mother, and she was also, apparently, quite a handful for her family—of whom I know, in fact, next to nothing, largely because my grandmother refuses to discuss her early years.

I do know that at sixteen my grandmother, whose family now lived on Gramercy Park, got pregnant, and that this was apparently the last straw for her family, who kicked her out of the house.

She then had the baby, my mother, on her own; and because she couldn't take care of the child, she took her to stay with a series of foster parents, and ultimately to Paterson, New Jersey, to a Catholic woman named Genevieve, with whom my mother spent her earliest years—a woman my mother has always remembered fondly.

Several years later, when my grandmother married Charles Marcus, a successful scientist and a vice president of Bendix Aviation, he said that he wanted both my mother and her younger half sister, Eleanor, who had been born during my grandmother's first, unsuccessful marriage to an N.Y.U. philosophy professor named Shephard, to take *his* name, which both my mother and Eleanor then did. Rosheen never, in fact, told her older daughter that she was illegitimate, and my mother always assumed that Shephard was her own as well as Eleanor's actual father. It wasn't until the night before I was born that she learned from Eleanor that this wasn't the case.

I don't know the circumstances of my father's finding out about my mother's illegitimacy or the fact that she was Jewish, but it must have been portentous to say the least for these two, after all, rather understandable deceptions to have assumed such monumental weight in his mind. But perhaps it only seems this way to me because I am myself, of course, half Jewish. And I was also conceived before my parents were married—at my father's insistence, to make sure that my mother could bear him children.

The rest of the items were minor in comparison to these three central deceptions. Nevertheless, he told me everything with the same emphasis of terrible, nightmarish frustration of the deepest instincts of his life. I remember standing on the first class deck of the ship, as he leaned against the rail and looked mournfully into the middle distance. Perhaps all these revelations were so important to me, after all, because they promised me a glimpse of the deeper reality of my father himself—a glimpse which, in fact, amidst all the smoke and fire of this endless tirade, was never to materialize.

My mother had no inner resources, he stressed to me,

with an implicit warning against any tendency I might find in myself not to be able to keep my mind and spirit and body—I am using words he himself was fond of—in proper harmony without all sorts of expensive distractions every minute.

She was a party girl. She wanted nothing but fun every minute, while he had to sweat through holy hell just to put food on the table.

She talked on the telephone as if her very life depended on it, as if her spirit itself would disintegrate if she couldn't, for hours at a time, employ this invention for its fulfillment.

She had nothing but rich and famous friends, but she herself was nothing more than a pathetic little nobody, a playgirl, barely better than a high-class harlot, if in fact she *was* any better.

He said he doubted (although he knew for a fact) that she had been a virgin when they met when she was scarcely seventeen years old. She seemed to know everybody, and she was awfully, awfully clever.

How he loved that word! It was probably the very worst thing he could say of another human being. And my mother, of course, was the cleverest of the clever. She knew how to do everything—everything, that is, but to be honest, be straight, be sincere, and tell the truth.

She used him viciously, sapped his strength, his money, his pride, his very ability to write, upon which we were all of us dependent.

She had once come upstairs into his office on the top floor of the house on Taraval Street in San Francisco, where they lived when I was three years old and Lucy had just been born—she had come upstairs and disturbed him while he was working, broken his rhythm, and, standing there, had picked up a piece of his work that lay on a table in his office. She had read a little of it, and then asked him what he was going to call it.

"I don't know," he answered in sincerity.

"Why don't you call it 'Shit,'" she suggested.

My father didn't mention to me here that they had seriously discussed his idea to use this title on a very good piece of work: that given such a context it would amount to an aesthetic breakthrough. On the contrary, a great man, before his thirteen-year-old son, was confessing the horrible torment of his life. My father nodded pensively into the distance here. It was that deep wayward streak in her coming out again and trying to destroy his hard-earned dignity.

Let me confess here that I have been torn all along in the above between wanting to lay out the details of what he told me with a more or less straightforward expository accuracy, and a simultaneous desire to cry out at the grim, smug, humorless, and finally horrifying inhumanity of every claim he made against my mother.

I have hesitated to do this because I realize how much more effective it would be if I could simply give him enough rope to hang himself, but I wonder now if it can be that easily accomplished.

For one thing, my father has, over the past twenty years, employing all the literary resources at his disposal, and I might add with all the considerable, indeed formidable, cleverness that he possesses, executed a full-scale multivolumed literary libel against my mother, who, for reasons of her own, and against the advice of others, has never lifted a finger to stop him.

This bitter, self-indulgent, unreciprocated and utterly deceitful attack would have amounted to more than a minor embarrassment to her, I suppose, and one which she would at some point have been obliged to meet head on in a legal proceeding, were it not for the fact that any such action would call far more attention to the writings in question than they have, without exception, otherwise received.*

But, at the same time, William Saroyan is still something in the nature of an American public legend, and I'm afraid that a reader might find this legend attractive enough to want to keep it intact in the face of a simple presentation of all these facts.

After all, taking my father at his word, wasn't it horrible for her to say that about calling it "Shit"—? Yes, let's suppose it *was* horrible. But on the other hand, as anyone knows who has ever been a husband in a household with small children for more than two or three weeks, it was exactly that moment to crack up laughing—because it was also funny, in a way typical of an exhausted young mother—and knock off for the day, get a baby-sitter, and take the poor woman out for dinner.

Not having done that, a decade later my father looked out to sea and went on berating my mother to me; my sad beleaguered father, who had in the meantime grown the large walrus mustache of an old-country patriarch, as

*My mother did, in fact, after two full decades of abuse, finally have her revenge. It occurred on the night of April 4, 1978 on *The Barbara Walters Special* on network television. Interviewed with her husband of the past twenty years, Walter Matthau, she was asked by Walters what she thought of her first husband, William Saroyan, whereupon she broke into a spontaneous diatribe, beginning "I *hate* him. He's a man straitjacketed by his own poisons . . . ," while her husband, as if to honor the equal-time ruling, recited in back of her what amounted to the substance of my father's public legend—"Bill's a great writer. He's a wonderful father," etc.—with which she was playing no uncertain havoc. It was electrifying television, and, for me, seeing my mother get and *take* her long-deferred day in court, a moment worth cheering.

if, having in reality failed to become a family man, he would henceforth become a sort of walking advertisement for the condition at its outmoded extreme.

This mustache first appears, in fact, at around the time of his first divorce from my mother. It is there on the back-cover photograph of a book called *Rock Wagram,* a book about a movie star whose marriage is cracking up, but in fact one largely made up of my father's not quite genuinely novelistic projection of himself as a good and troubled man. ("Every man is a good man in a bad world," the book begins.) The mustache, which, in this first incarnation, is as large and as little integrated into the architecture of my father's face as an old-country mustache in a college play, is accompanied by an expression (I see it before me now as I write) which is a bold attempt, but one that I find it nevertheless impossible not to see through, at the proud, quixotic look of an old-country peasant looking directly out into a world gone mad.

This would be a stance my father would henceforth refine, along with the mustache itself, for the rest of his life.

Last night I read a chunk of this chronicle to Gailyn and the kids, all of us equally, in our own ways, trying to metabolize the reality of my father's dying. Each morning I get up early with my mind a continuing torrent, but except for the first day—almost a week ago now—when Strawberry's tears released some of my own, there has been only a stray shudder and a stray flicker of emotion (the shudder one day; the flicker another) and last night Gailyn said outright, puzzled by her own grappling for a response to this normally emotionally simple time: "You hate your father."

And I was surprised and put off somewhat by so simple and clear-cut a declaration of what is surely, in some sense, at least a *part* of the truth. But I must say, in all fairness to what is happening to me in this prolonged moment, that I believe there is far more here than simple hatred, and in fact I don't believe that is even the greater part of it.

I admitted to Gailyn last night that I was, most likely, *relieved* above all by his dying. And almost at once after admitting this, I said that I believe my mother, and then, even longer than she, Lucy and I, have kept him alive as long as he has, in fact, lived. And the corollary of this: that my refusal to see him or write him or in any way make further contact with him contributed to his death —that it was, finally, the most killing thing I could have done to him.

*   *   *

"Tell Aram if he comes here," he told Lucy, "he'll kill me." Or if he writes or if he phones. Perhaps Lucy and my mother and I have in a certain sense always killed him —that is, we have brought his poisons to the surface; we have unfrozen him.

I remember my father once saying to me on the phone, "You've set me back a day already." How, exactly, had I done this? And how did he know it was a day exactly that he had been set back—and from where?

It seems clear to me now that he was speaking of this unfreezing—always mechanistically accompanied by screaming—of his emotional life.

For there was, simply, no way in the world that this three-year-old child could have metabolized emotionally the death of his father and mother (in all but the literal sense for the following five years), and in order to survive, as I have said, I believe he put himself emotionally on ice. The lake went hard.

And the screaming, the emotional agony of really the whole of my father's marriage to my mother, nevertheless I believe represented, physiologically and psychically, the healthy sign that the psyche was at last feeling the pain of its long frozen contents, that these were in fact now at large within the body and spirit as a whole.

But this was, most likely, of a deep, very possibly entirely overwhelming order of pain; and it must have been, too, almost impossibly confusing for my father, who, having fallen in love with my mother, suddenly found himself experiencing the most severe emotional crisis of his life, something that in a man less strong in his hold on his own interior life would have led directly to a nervous breakdown. Had this happened, in fact, and had he then recovered from it, he might have then emerged as a truly new man, one who had finally unfrozen in himself, and at last accepted and then triumphed over his early pain.

But, considering the whole nature of the time and the event itself, this seems almost too much to hope for. Not only was my mother a young and inexperienced woman in a situation that would most likely have proved an impossible trial for the most evolved woman imaginable, but my father himself seems to have had no conscious sense whatsoever of the specific source of his pain, and although a gifted and naturally intuitive artist, he seems to have decided almost immediately to blame my mother for what was going on inside him. And he then proceeded to find the reasons why he felt the way he felt: she was a liar who hadn't told him she was illegitimate and Jewish; she was falsely represented as an heiress, etc. And he continued to scream at her, eventually through my sister and me, for the rest of his life.

I believe it kept him alive. It was a simple relief action, this screaming.

Unhappily, however, there were very few people with whom he could indulge himself freely, and without embarrassment. There were really only three.

My mother, my sister, and me.

My mother had divorced him for the second time when I was eight. My sister had been largely out of touch with him for the past ten years.

That left me.

I had become a writer, married and started a family, and moved to a small town not far from San Francisco, where he occasionally stayed in his sister's house. And so, we saw each other for a while again, not often, once or twice a year, and he visited his grandchildren at the same time, until one afternoon on the phone, after I had done him a favor with regard to a property he owned in Malibu, advised him that he wasn't receiving enough rent on it, as well as other details I had dug up solely out of a sense of filial responsibility and affection, in the middle of our conversation, he suddenly blew up and screamed at me for half an hour—"When have you ever shown any business sense? You're a horse's ass!" etc.— and when I hung up, dazed, looking at my wife and children in front of me in the room, standing in the afternoon sunlight, I sensed that I was myself in mortal danger now from enduring any further such attacks from my father, that it was something like a choice between him or me, and that I had a wife and children to whom I owed my very deepest loyalty now—and so I decided to turn away from our relationship, and I took away any further option of his to scream at me.

In the end, perhaps it is pride that has been the deepest killer in my father's life, the *hubris* spoken of by the ancient Greeks, which made it impossible for him ever to let himself go, completely, to whatever fate the gods had in store for him, to surrender to his pain fully, rather than screaming that it was someone else's doing, and adopting a posture of outrage and anger before the particulars of his life—his young wife; his son; his daughter. (My mother has told me that the first time he saw me after he had returned from a year overseas in the army, he said to her only, "He looks Jewish.")

Getting help would have meant only a recognition that he himself, and not my mother (and later myself and my sister), was sick. There was, at this time, it is true, something of a bugaboo about the newly established profession of psychiatry: people spoke of the possibility that an artist who submitted himself to psychoanalysis might, in the process of trying to achieve psychic health, lose his talent; and this is the sort of hearsay I can imagine making a real impression on him. He was an almost purely intuitive artist, that is, and hence he wasn't above this sort of parochialism.

It was also just before the war was to transform the country entirely and his moment as a national literary hero was to pass. However, when my father met and fell in love with my mother, he was still riding high on the crest of his fame, although perhaps in his deeper thoughts he was aware that some sort of fundamental change was going on.

There were, after all, strong signs even then. After becoming a sensation in the American theater with his two plays, *My Heart's in the Highlands* in 1938 and *The Time of Your Life* in 1939 (for which he won the Pulitzer Prize he declined), two free-form jazzlike improvisations that repeated on the stage the magic he had achieved in the pages of his early stories—after these two clear-cut successes (and *both* plays won the Drama Critics Award for the Best Play), he then had several more plays done, even establishing a Saroyan Theater on Broadway to produce a number of them himself, and none of these plays had either the critical or the commercial success of his first two plays, most of them amounting to more or less distinguished flops.

Was he losing his touch?

He also spoke to me once of a phenomenon that occurred during this same period of his life. He told me that up until the age of thirty-five, the age in fact at which he met my mother, he had been able to wake up at the crack of dawn each morning, write a short story, take a walk, bet the horses, hang out in bars and coffeehouses, get caught up in nightly parties and other adventures that might only end with his reaching bed by two or three in the morning, whereupon he would fall immediately into a sound sleep, from which he would awake once again at the crack of dawn, ready, willing, and able to repeat the whole cycle all over again.

But when he reached thirty-five, he told me, one morning when he hit the shower, he didn't feel his old immediate zest and eagerness to begin the day, but instead felt beat and dead and hung over, wanting only to crawl back into his bed—and he did, in fact, at this time, visit a doctor who simply told him that he couldn't expect his body to perform in this way, at least not any longer, day after day and night after night, and that henceforth when he stayed up late at night he should expect to sleep later into the morning.

My mother, on the other hand, has told me that my father is the only man she has ever known who would spend literally *days* resting in his bed, during the years of their marriage. This, by itself, might indicate something of the psychic conflict in which he found himself during his marriage. But the degree to which his involvement with my mother affected this departure from his former, pre-thirty-five-year-old daily routine, and how much of it was simply the result of the onset of his middle life on top of the fact of the normal adjustment of married life, is most likely impossible to reckon except very broadly. It seems clear that everything happened at once.

I do wonder, though, if the onset of his middle life didn't, in effect, make him both more vulnerable to and at the same time more needful of a full-fledged experience of "falling in love" than he had ever before been.

What I am saying is that as his body had assumed its mature rhythm, and he had slowed down, at last, from the seemingly nonstop pace of his youth, hadn't he, in effect, found himself in need of some new form of vital sustenance? It was during this time, in fact, that his weight was to become a recurrent problem.

For his style, in effect, *was* youth. He was a writer who spoke with a kind of self-amazed delight of his own ability to write a short story in a few hours, a whole play, like *The Time of Your Life,* in six days—as if it were his nervous system that he was really celebrating, at least in a certain sense, in these works, the life-force itself as it was embodied in the variety of forms of his writing.

The Time of Your Life is an amazing achievement of this order. It is a play approaching the order of a jazz dance, in which the words themselves are part of an overall choreography, a shifting from one part of the stage to another, that infects one with the same *physical* sense of pleasure that is usually the unique domain of music.

It is almost as if, having by necessity cut himself off from his own deepest emotional fluency, but having nonetheless emerged with both a sound mind and a strong body, as well as developing an intuitive, natural sense of touch as an artist, he then cast around almost *at random* for his subject matter—through the sad and sometimes gaudy streets of Depression-sunk San Francisco—and whatever he found became the *vehicle* for his real story. Or, in fact, it is more likely a kind of poem he happened to write in prose, which was Youth itself, the sap rising up through him each morning as he sat before his typewriter with his cup of coffee, as he inhaled and exhaled on a Chesterfield—and wasn't this, in its own way, something very close to love and immortality?

He was a young prose writer, that is, who did something characteristic of young poets. He wrote with a purity and profundity from the depths of his own nervous system, celebrating less in narrative than in sustained, jazzlike song what it was like to be young.

He was a man who held within him a mirror, which had crystallized and turned hard out of the unbearable fluids of his emotion as a three-year-old orphan, and that mirror was made out of the vision of his three-year-old self, an in fact awesome clarity of vision which is the property of the child. And perhaps the warp in the mirror was only that it was hard rather than fluid, and this in fact would ensure that its clarity would remain intact: that he would register youth's trajectory through him with a pure joy, unqualified by any more vulnerable emotion.

Yesterday morning, my father's cousin Harry Bagdasarian, who has been doing his shopping for him these past months and helping him out generally, phoned my father, and when there was no answer, he went over to his house to see if he was all right.

The previous morning, Sunday, he had done the same thing. It has been his daily procedure, in fact, to phone my father each morning and find out if he needs or wants anything ("Well, why don't you come over about eleven," my father would say to him, Harry told me over the phone yesterday). And when he drove over on Sunday morning, he found my father still asleep in his bed, but perfectly all right.

Yesterday, when he drove over and went into the house, he found my father sitting at a table with his head lying on the surface of the table. He was unconscious.

He phoned another of my father's cousins, Ruben Saroyan, the man Lucy spoke with outside the house, who has been doing gardening work for my father for the past five years, and he came over and the two put my father into his bed where, Harry told me, he looked much better than he had when Harry first saw him slumped over the table.

Later in our conversation, I asked Harry whether he had seen our scrapbook in the house—wanting to know whether my father had seen it before he had fallen unconscious—and he said yes, it had been on the table, as if it had recently arrived and he had opened the envelope and looked at it.

The first news I had of this change in my father's condition came yesterday around lunchtime, after I had stopped writing and gotten out of bed and was finishing eating some lunch I had made. Dr. Jibelian called to let me know he was about to go over to my father's house to examine him, and that his condition had now changed. The doctor wasn't sure if he was still unconscious or not.

I told the doctor that if my father *were* unconscious, I would like to come up and stay with him. The doctor had suggested that he might live only a few more hours—or, possibly, it could be a few more days.

If he had regained consciousness, or if this seemed likely, I wouldn't, of course, go up to stay with him, since he had made it very clear that he didn't want to see me. I asked the doctor when he would be back in his office, after examining my father, and he said in about an hour and a half. I said that I would phone him again then, at three.

I called Lucy to give her the news, and during the conversation, I asked her if she didn't want to meet me in Fresno, if Pop *were,* in fact, unconscious.

"Oh no, Ar," she said. "I'm not going back there. I'll never go back there as long as I live."

I took a bath and shaved for the first time in several days, while Gailyn put some clothes into an overnight bag for me, as well as ironing three of my shirts—something I can't remember her doing before.

Then I drove downtown with Cream and Armenak— Cream was staying home from school, and Armenak goes to preschool only from Tuesday through Friday—to do some shopping and get the mail, and to kill the time left before three o'clock when I would call the doctor.

We visited the library briefly, but when I checked the time and found that it was close to three, I called to the kids, who were in the Children's Books section, that it was time to leave, and we checked out a book and then drove back up to the house.

When I called Dr. Jibelian, he told me my father was unconscious but was breathing, although there was some congestion—that he'd possibly had a stroke, and that they had decided to admit him to the Veterans Administration Hospital in Fresno.

I told him that I wanted to come up and stay with my father so that he could die at home, as I assumed he wanted to do. The doctor said that my father was concerned about not having strong medication, so-called "heroic measures," such as chemotherapy and radiation, but that he hadn't said anything specifically regarding dying at home. I said that it seemed clear to me that since he didn't want any strong medication, and I wanted to come up and stay with him, there was no reason for him to be sent to the hospital.

"Well, he's already gone," he told me.

"He's already been moved from the house?"

"I think so—he should be by now."

He said that he and Ruben and Harry had discussed it and decided that this would be the best thing to do. I didn't argue with the doctor because I wanted to call Pop's house right away to try to stop them if he hadn't yet been moved, and tell them that I would be coming up. I had to get my father's telephone number from the doctor, as well as Harry Bagdasarian's and Ruben Saroyan's.

I called my father's house and no one answered.

I called Harry Bagdasarian and there was no answer.

I called Ruben Saroyan, too, and no one answered there, either.

Then I called the Veterans Administration Hospital. After my call was transferred to Admissions, and then to Nurses, it was determined that my father had just arrived at "Four East" in the hospital. I spoke to his nurse there, identifying myself as my father's son and his next of kin, and saying that he had been sent to the hospital against his own wishes, and that I wanted him to be taken back to his house—that I was coming up to be with him so he could die at home.

Somehow, it seemed important for me to do this, perhaps the final gesture of goodwill I could send to my father before he reached his grave.

Once, in the late fifties, when I had started high school in Manhattan, my father came into town and stayed in a room at the Hotel Royalton, which eventually became his regular hotel in New York. It was the hotel, on West Forty-fourth Street between Fifth and Sixth avenues, where his old friend, the theater critic George Jean Nathan, was now dying, attended to daily by Julie Haydon, the actress who had played Kitty Duval in *The Time of Your Life*.

When I got to my father's room, one dark New York winter afternoon, during which everything seemed to have turned to varying shades of deep gray, I found him sick in his bed, a situation I don't remember ever seeing him in before—or since.

Why do I remember it at this particular moment?

The problem was that I didn't know what was happening to my father, whether he merely had a serious cold or was at death's door, and I believe that my father, rather than simply making an assessment of his condition to me, one way or the other, so that we could both then take the next logical step—whether medicine from the drugstore needed to be bought, or an ambulance sent for —chose instead, with what I now can regard only as sly and in fact cruel calculation, to keep me in a state of suspense, bordering on panic, during the remainder of the afternoon.

How did he do this?

He was, lying in his bed, unshaven and with hair disheveled, suddenly and uniquely almost inarticulate. I couldn't quite get him to tell me just what was wrong with him, even when I would say things to him like, "Do you think you might be really sick, Pop? I mean *really* sick—maybe needing a hospital, a bout of pneumonia, maybe, something that, if you don't do something about it now, could maybe even lead to your dying?"—I mean I was getting very dramatic, and rather frightened, and more and more full of momentous urgency. Nevertheless, he remained, for the first and last time in all the years I have known him, almost bovine in what I now regard as a completely feigned inability to tell me what was going on.

And yet, at the same time, he probably sensed in me, quite correctly, a real need, if not in fact an overwhelming hunger, to make some form of emotional contact with him—something that forever seemed to elude me —to the point where I myself was a bit too eager, just a bit too ready to carry this somewhat ambiguous situation, but perhaps not one necessarily a catalyst for a major drama—to carry this vision of my father sick in his bed right to the edge of life and death itself.

I wanted, rather desperately, an emotional quickening of terms in our relationship. I wanted, just once, a moment in which I could, with some genuine sense of my own value to him, do something that I knew answered some actual need that he had. I wanted, in effect, to be both his son and his friend—which was, of course, just what I wanted yesterday as he lay very literally at death's door.

I remember riding the elevator at the Royalton to get him something he had asked for—aspirin perhaps, or maybe just a candy bar and a newspaper—and looking suddenly wide-eyed at everything, straining toward some kind of emotional consummation which, in fact, was never to arrive. As the afternoon turned into evening, it became clear to me that nothing was really going to happen, or not through me, anyway, although my father was never quite willing to say to me, "I'll be all right, Aram. No need to get too excited—it's just the flu or something."

And yesterday I was still straining after the same thing, and yet now half of me was already resigned to the fact that there would be no emotional consummation whatsoever.

He was lying peacefully in his bed at the hospital, breathing with some congestion, but nothing as yet severe. Dr. Jensen-Akula, who was taking care of him now, and who had been seeing him previously along with Dr. Jibelian, assured me that his desire not to have medication would be honored. He was unconscious, and responded in no way except if his finger was pricked, which meant that he still could feel pain.

I told the doctor what I wanted to do, which was agreeable to him, but after two more phone calls—one to Dr. Jibelian again, and the other to Hospice, which provided no around-the-clock home-care service in Fresno—it seemed clear to me that I had, in fact, made a mistake.

"Why didn't you phone me before you made the decision to send him to the hospital?" I asked Dr. Jibelian, a quiet and gentle-voiced man.

"Well, your father . . ." he hesitated here. "Your father said he didn't want to see you . . . in the condition he is in."

"He actually told you that?"

"Yes," he said. "He did."

"But I told you I'd only come up if he was unconscious. Is there some chance that he might revive?"

"I don't think so, no," Dr. Jibelian answered.

"Well then, I'll come up and stay with him in the house."

He said that if I wanted to do that, it would be all right with him, but that it was a big job, around the clock. If he wet his bed, it had to be changed, and so on.

Suddenly I saw myself simultaneously lifting my father out of his bed, so that I could change it, and terrified that he might regain consciousness and go crazy when he saw me.

The final possibility was Hospice, having someone there with me so that, should he regain consciousness, I could quickly get out of the room.

And now, suddenly, it all seemed laughable. This pious filial effort on my part, hinging in the first place entirely on my father's being unconscious, and on his not regaining consciousness, in order that I might do for him what was in my heart.

What a fool I am! I thought. With my irrelevant pieties, when the man would very likely be repelled, for all I know, if I touched his hand while he slept.

The doctor had said that my father had never made any mention of having an around-the-clock nurse, a service available, though not through Hospice, which specializes in seeing families through home deaths in something of the way doctors and midwives now attend home births.

But all of a sudden I knew that my father would prefer being in the hospital to any more intimate setup, and I realized that everything was proceeding, in fact, most likely just exactly as he wanted it.

Even at death's door, he would refuse the father and son amenities. He had had no father, and it was his son who was supposed to die. If it became clear, as it had, that he himself was to die before his son, he would still be able to arrange his death in such a way that it appeared, at least to him, that he had no son after all.

This morning I drove Armenak down to the Bolinas School—Gailyn coming along for the ride—where everyone is meeting today, before taking off on a field trip to the Audubon Canyon Ranch, on the other side of the lagoon from us. He seemed in good spirits as we drove, not really aware of the drama unfolding in all our lives. He hadn't in fact seen his Grandpa Bill since infancy.

When we got back to the house, after a stop at the grocery story and the post office, I called the hospital. Dr. Jensen-Akula told me that Pop had spontaneously revived overnight, and was now conscious again.

It's a good thing I didn't go up.

The doctor said that, although now conscious, he was very confused—he apparently wanted a glass of water, which the doctor got for him—and still very weak from what appears to have been a stroke.

Yesterday afternoon, I received a phone call from the hospital after I had phoned them to say that I wouldn't, after all, be coming up to move my father. A secretary phoned to tell me that my cousin Arnold Papazian, the son of my father's sister Zabe, had just visited the hospital and left his card for me. But the real reason for the call, she explained to me, was that a staff member at the hospital had heard Arnold speaking to the man he had come in with—who turned out to be Ruben Saroyan—saying something about getting a van and going to my father's house and taking stuff out of it.

My cousin Arnold is a big man, now in his middle forties, a successful businessman in Salinas, who has always been friendly and easy-natured, one of my favorite relatives, and one of Lucy's, too. I haven't seen him, however, in the last six or seven years, and the last time we saw one another, we found ourselves somewhat ill at ease, and we ended up in an argument about César Chavez—Arnold against him for business reasons—that didn't do either of us any good.

The phone call from the hospital set in motion a series of my own calls that lasted the remainder of the day and into the night, and by the end of it, I had spoken with Harry Bagdasarian, Ruben Saroyan, my father's cousin, the poet Archie Minasian (who had driven up to Fresno that day to see Pop, only to find him unconscious at the hospital), my father's brother, Henry, and Arnold himself. I also spoke with my mother.

I haven't seen my father's Fresno houses in sixteen years—he has *two* houses, one on the corner and one right next to it, in a middle-income housing development—but I wasn't surprised to learn yesterday on the phone, from both Harry and Arnold, that both of these houses, like-every other house he has lived in, but these now even more so, are filled in some places to the point of being impossible to walk through, with books, papers, and boxes primarily, but also with numberless line drawings and watercolors, rocks, and coins. He sometimes fills a Mason jar with either rocks or coins, seals it, and sets it on a desk or bureau.

Once, when I visited my father's downstairs studio

apartment at my aunt's house in San Francisco at a time when he himself wasn't staying there—this was a period, in the late sixties, just after Gailyn and I had gotten married and I had hair down to my shoulders and scarcely anything in my wallet—I was almost prompted to grab a jar of coins off his bureau and bolt past my seventy-year-old aunt—who wasn't sure she was supposed to allow me into his basement apartment in the first place—and run for the door.

But I didn't, I wasn't even halfway serious about it in fact, but only marveled at this construction: here was money that had been taken out of circulation, money that had been purposefully taken out of currency, and frozen in time and space inside a glass jar, although if I took it and ran, it would buy stuff; quarters and fifty-cent pieces were in there, enough to buy several days' worth of food and shelter, or just luxury items, dinners or movies, books, records. I saw this jar, in fact, at a time when it would strike me with particular poignancy since I seemed to have decided to let a smile be my umbrella, with of course less than perfect success, and the money in the jar would, at that moment, certainly have provided a service-able umbrella.

And this construction has haunted me somehow ever since: a sealed Mason jar, filled to the brim with American coins.

I ask myself now if this isn't, in fact, a rather perfect symbolic embodiment of the very condition in my father that I have been trying to characterize all along. It is, quite simply, real money, but sealed in a jar. It is frozen assets.

And next to it on the bureau sat another sealed Mason jar, filled to the brim with rocks.

And what of these rocks in the jar?

This seems to me now an interesting, and equally revealing, more or less complementary variation on the same theme. Instead of money behind the glass, here there are rocks; and the two jars stood side by side on his bureau, two identical containers, as if, in effect, they belonged together, were to be taken as a unit, a single expression.

"Time is money," the old truism goes; and isn't money *locked up* in a jar, in turn, like a form of pure time, untranslatable into space—or, as I think of it, into earthly dimensions of pleasure? It is "hard cash" which will never, so long as it is locked up in a glass jar, translate itself into anything "softer," and in doing so, of course, spend itself.

My mother's most characteristic and enduring description of my father over the years has been that he is an "emotional miser," a phrase I find myself remembering now, if only because it seems so aptly to encapsulate at least one dimension of the symbolic self-portrait I believe my father intuitively conceived in the two jars set side by side.

I don't mean to be coy in bringing this up, as if I am holding back my own anger at what is absolutely an emotional truth about my father, but at this moment I would only like to mention the phrase in connection with the jars themselves, because they seem to embody such a symbolic storehouse of information.

The rocks, of course, cannot translate into anything at all. They are simply themselves: the most enduring known form of matter. In their own way, and from the opposite direction, as it were, they too approach the condition of pure time, as untranslatable into softer, earthly pleasures as the sealed jar of money.

*   *   *

And what, exactly, might "pure time" be?

Could it be time that is in no way impeded, or wasted, or spent in its interaction with space? Could it be, in this sense, perhaps a kind of equivalent, in my father's mind, for eternity or immortality itself?

"An immortal day," my father wrote in the book he inscribed to Aram Kevorkian. A day which will, I suppose, be remembered forever, or at least as long as my father and Aram are, either of them, alive to remember it.

Or is it possible that my father believes that it will last even longer than that, and, if so, how would that be possible?

It occurs to me that it would only be possible if my father believed that he had some kind of means, in himself, to live beyond death, to continue to exist in that state of pure time of the rocks and the money sealed in the glass jars.

My cousin Arnold, with whom I had a warm conversation on the phone last night after he had returned from Fresno, where he had seen my father unconscious at the hospital, described the Fresno houses, which he has visited many times, as "raggedy-shack." They are filled to bursting, as I've said, with my father's "collections": books that he has largely picked up for nickels and dimes in used bookstores and which largely go unread, as well as newer books publishers and writers send him; boxes containing filled manila envelopes, usually addressed to him, which are, for the most part, each signed and dated by my father; correspondence, of course, including carbon copies of every letter he himself has written; magazines (often stored in boxes); a red page-a-day series of diaries for each year since 1938 to the present; very likely

thousands of line drawings, often done on hotel stationery and invariably signed, though sometimes only with
the initials "WS," and dated, very often including the
exact time at which the drawing was completed; abstract
watercolors on larger sheets of paper, some of these care-
lessly framed in ready-made dime-store frames and hung
on the walls; and other less extensive, but no doubt in no
way less important, collections—important, that is, to my
father himself.

Arnold had suggested at the hospital that if my father
were to die, and hence the news of his death to make the
media rounds, all of this material should be moved to a
warehouse to avoid having any of it vandalized before it
is sorted: a sound idea, I think. For there is also, of
course, an enormous amount of published and unpublished original manuscript material—he has at least as
many unpublished manuscripts as he has published books
(fifty or more to date)—and this work would of course
have an immediate cash value in the literary-archive mar-
ketplace.

In addition to all of these collections, over the past
twenty years, my father's published books themselves
have tended to take the form of "collections" of memories, each chapter amounting to a re-creation of an event
or personality or place, or combinations thereof, that has
remained in his memory. The books are often arranged
around a particular, if necessarily rather broad theme,
which in most cases is reflected in their titles: *Chance
Meetings, Places Where I Have Done Time, Letters from 74
Rue Taitbout* (letters from his Paris apartment to people,
from immortals to unknowns, who have died), *Sons Come
& Go, Mothers Hang In Forever* (memories of the great,
near great, and not at all great—including, of course, my
mother)—and finally, and most recently, an unusual

book called *Obituaries.* Each chapter of this book is a single paragraph of several pages—each chapter a kind of tombstone itself—devoted to my father's memories of an individual listed in *Variety*'s annual list of deaths for 1976.

My mind strains after the logic—or, more likely, the magic—implicit in these "collections." There is a consistent, if to me still less than transparent, inner necessity behind all of them. I believe my father is engaged in some sort of fundamental ritual in "holding on" to all of this stuff, getting it down on paper, or into envelopes, or into boxes, or into jars, so that it will not be discarded, so that it will last, and not be thrown away or otherwise be "spent," and disappear.

It is not uncommon, for instance, to find a manila envelope in one of his houses—Gailyn and I once examined a box of them in his apartment in Paris, when we stayed there a few months after we had met, in the late fall of 1967—a manila envelope, carefully signed and dated, in which, for instance, the only contents are flyers from a travel agency he apparently stopped at on a walk that day. Perhaps he was considering a trip?

This is possible, of course, but what of another envelope, also signed and dated, and with a line drawing in his perennial style—a single, intersecting, interpenetrating line, all curves, begun in one place and ended in another: time itself?—an envelope containing a slew of pamphlets devoted to the tide cycles in North Africa during 1965, as well as a freebie on custom shampoos and haircuts for dogs (my father has never in his adult life, so far as I know, had a pet of any kind), and a large and untouched stack of stationery from the Hotel Ritz in Paris?

Or what of his diaries dating back to 1938, the year he

turned thirty, in which he deals minutely with physical processes such as getting up (exact time), showering, shaving, writing a story, eating breakfast, walking, picking up groceries and laundry, eating lunch, stopping at a bookie joint, etc., until getting to bed that night (exact time)? These books are, likewise, "collections" of events that would otherwise be consigned to oblivion, given the permanent status of literary notation, however perfunctory.

What is my father doing here?

I believe that he is, essentially, writing his name over and over and over again, and that these signatures, in form of the boxes and envelopes, Mason jars and drawings, are all ways of telling himself that he has continued to stay alive, that he is still, up to that moment, "not dying"; and, at the same time, that these signatures—comprising what, with the exception of the jar of money (and even this is, after all, "small change"), are usually considered highly ephemeral and inconsequential items—amount to a kind of *willed* immortality.

At the same time, when you consider all of this material in its in fact rather awesome entirety, it is as if he is giving us a kind of enormous, mixed-media self-portrait, perhaps the major work of his lifetime—his last will and testament, his final and deepest claim to immortality itself—and the one by which, if I am not mistaken, through his actual will, he intends to freeze his assets beyond the grave itself, rather than have them pass through the normal channels of inheritance.

He has, in effect, I believe, come up with a way to "hold on" to his money and all of his other "collections" even after death, so that, for all intents and purposes, he will still be Not Dying—a way in which he himself, by force of his own will, in both senses of the word, can "guarantee" himself immortality.

Armenak Saroyan at thirty-three.
New York, 1907.

Zabelle, Takoohi, Henry, Armenak,
and Cosette Saroyan. New York, 1907.

Zabelle, Henry, William, and Cosette Saroyan.
California, 1910?

Henry and William Saroyan. Campbell, 1911.
Just after Armenak's death.

William Saroyan. San Francisco, 1934.
(Photograph by Willard Van Dyke.)

William Saroyan and George Jean Nathan. New York, 1940.

Carol Marcus. New York, 1944.
(Photograph by G. Maillard Kesslere.)

Carol Saroyan, Rosheen Marcus, Aram Saroyan.
New York, 1944. (Photograph by G. Maillard Kesslere.)

Bill and Carol (pregnant with Lucy). Fresno, 1945.

Bill and Carol. August 7, 1947 at the
Fairmont Hotel in San Francisco.

Carol, Lucy, and Aram. New York, 1949.
(Photograph by Milton Greene.)

Aram and Lucy in Beverly Hills, 1951, during
the second marriage. (Photograph by Jean Howard.)

William and Aram Saroyan. San Francisco, 1964.
(Photograph by Archie Minasian.)

William Saroyan with his grandchildren:
from left, Cream, Armenak, and Strawberry.
Bolinas, 1977. (Photograph by Aram Saroyan.)

William Saroyan at his will signing on October 21, 1980 in Fresno. His witnesses are (standing, from left) Dr. Harold Haack, president of California State University at Fresno; Dickran Kouymjian, coordinator of the Armenian Studies Program at CSUF; Richard Harrington, Saroyan's lawyer at the time; (seated, from left) Leon Peters, chairman of the Fresno Foundation of CSUF; Allan Jendian, acting chairman of the Ad Hoc Steering Committee of the Armenian National Museum; and Marvin Baxter, lawyer for the Armenian National Museum and Cultural Center.

Archie Minasian and William Saroyan. Fresno,
March, 1981. (Photograph by Helen Minasian.)

As I understand it, and it is not unexpected because he has spoken alternately of a Saroyan Foundation or a Saroyan Library for the past fifteen years, my father plans to arrange for the major portion of his estate to endow an institution bearing his own name, which will house and in fact serve as a kind of self-styled and self-perpetuated museum for every bit of the material that I have just discussed, and of course a great deal more. In the garage at his sister Cosette's house, for instance, he has a complete or near complete set of the old *Life* magazine, and many of the early issues of *Esquire,* as well as less extensive collections of other magazines.

Arnold told me over the phone that Ruben Saroyan had told him that my father had changed his will over and over again during this past year or so, and Ruben reported to him with regard to what I assume to be the current will, to which Ruben was apparently a witness, that all of my father's real-estate properties—his two houses in Fresno, his Paris apartment, and his beachhouse in Malibu—are to become, in one form or another, part of the Saroyan Foundation. (This is, as Arnold emphasized, in the nature of hearsay, but somehow not unexpected to me.)

My father's beachhouse at Malibu which he bought at the time of the second divorce for, as I remember, something like $17,000, has over the past ten years been allowed to deteriorate to the point that when I visited the property in September of 1980, the county had posted a notice of a hearing to show cause why the building should not be removed. This is the house I had advised him on, which led to his explosion over the phone.

As I understand it, since what remains of the building after the rain slides of the last several years is either of no value in itself, or has now in fact been removed by the county, this property, which is now worth in the neighborhood of half a million dollars for its site alone—Malibu is simply the least smog-bound area of Los Angeles—is to be sold, and the proceeds split between the Saroyan Foundation and my Aunt Cosette, in whose name it had originally been bought by my father (most likely to avoid a lien by the Internal Revenue Service), and whose major source of income it had been before it became too run-down to rent.

My Aunt Cosette, now eighty-two, is a very dear woman. But it became obvious to me, in our weekly Sunday telephone conversations several years ago, that her almost saintly generosity of spirit had found an unworthy recipient in her current tenant at Malibu, a man whom she was charging a monthly figure less than half of what she could get (a figure that barely in fact covered her taxes on the place) and who even so was chronically late with the rent—which, when it became overdue by a month or more, put both an emotional and financial strain on my aunt, who was recovering from an expensive eye operation.

It also became clear to me that her tenant had discovered that his landlady's goodwill and credulity were of truly prodigious dimensions, and that by periodically calling her with excuses relating to his own personal hopes and trials, he could put off paying her almost indefinitely. It was at this point that I wrote my father of this situation, suggesting to him that 1) the tenant's lease, which was up for renewal, not be renewed, and that 2) the rent be doubled.

My father, because of his own schedule—including, as I remember, an imminent writers' conference in Bulgaria —was not able to see to these matters, and never in fact answered or acknowledged my letter at all.

This is significant, I think, because it was a moment when I might very literally have been able to do something useful for him. It was also a moment which might, however slightly, have stirred him at the deeper levels of his being, nearing seventy, as he was, with a grown-up son who was now offering help in a family matter: this just for a moment, perhaps, might have caused something in the nature of an unfreezing in my father—which, of course, would then cause him pain.

In any case, unlike any other letter I sent him during this period, this one he chose not to answer, and, as I said, not to acknowledge specifically at all, although I heard from Cosette that he had discussed the situation with her.

The tenant, then, knowing that his lease was about to expire, and hoping to renew it, managed both to pay up his rent due and to call my aunt asking for a renewal without a significant rent hike. When he got this, he was then able to sign and seal this agreement with the necessary first and last month's rent.

My father went off to Bulgaria, and then to Paris, where he usually spent his spring and summer.

By the time he returned I was aware, having talked to my aunt each Sunday on the phone, that the tenant had not in fact paid one more month's rent after his initial payment with the new lease, and that my aunt, so long as he continued to prey on her sense of Christian charity, would be more or less constitutionally incapable of taking any action, although her own financial situation, with taxes owed both on her house in San Francisco and on the Malibu place, was at a crisis point. I wrote to my father, now back in Fresno, and told him these details, both financial and psychological, and suggested that the solution at this point would be to serve the tenant with an eviction notice.

Again my father made no reply to my letter, and never acknowledged it in any phone conversation I had with him; but I heard from my aunt some time later that the tenant had been served an eviction notice.

The tenant occupied the beachhouse for ten months before being evicted. When he left he had paid only the first and last months' rent. The money he owed was never, subsequently, recovered. And after he was out, when the house was examined by a relative living in Los Angeles, it was found to be so much in disrepair that it couldn't be rented again until it had been put in order.

It was at around this time that I had what was to be my final telephone conversation with my father. The circumstances were quite simply as I have written. It occurred to me that he might want to visit, since he was in San Francisco at the time, and I called him to invite him. Either I spoke to him then, or—I can't quite remember which—he was out at the time, and he returned my call when he got back and Cosette gave him the message that I'd called.

My own state of mind at the time was quite good, as I remember. I thought that I might be able to give him my help in getting the Malibu place fixed up again. I was going to suggest to him that perhaps I could go down and oversee the repairs for him and Cosette. It would be an opportunity for me to get away for a few days.

I was also expecting, rather foolishly I now see, something in the nature of casual thanks from my father for getting on the case with the Malibu place, and staying with it over the past year or more. The tenant was now out, and it had been largely my own assessments of the situation that had been acted on—or, when ignored, as in the case of renewing the tenant's lease, it had proved to be a mistake.

I knew of course that my father was not going to make very much of my efforts, but at the same time, just in having carried through the little that I did do, I was aware on some level, though not quite conscious of it, that in this admittedly small, more or less stumbled-upon arena, our relationship had in fact undergone a quiet but significant turn, if not in fact *the* turn that I had been wanting, and somehow had never quite been able to achieve, almost from the beginning. I had finally, I felt, been able to do something, however small, that might simply prove to have been useful to him.

Our telephone conversation, as I remember, started off on an easy note, if at the same time I sensed a certain restless unease at the bottom of it that hadn't been in our usual telephone talks. It was also true that this time *I* was inviting him out, whereas it normally seemed to be at his instigation that his visits were planned and carried through. But he quickly declined my invitation, with thanks and regrets, pleading, probably quite genuinely, lack of time—although, in retrospect, I can't help but feel that there were other more directly personal urgencies under this impersonal one.

As my father lies dying now, three and a half years later, I realize I am speaking of simply the very last direct communication I ever had with him, after which I never again either saw or spoke to him, and only once again heard from him directly in any form—the letter I received from him after my car accident, which occurred half a year later.

I remember talking with my mother the other night on the telephone, and telling her it had suddenly come to me why Pop had acted as he had all these years. My mother, to whom the trivial points of departure for his screaming tirades must have been not just deeply unsettling but of a different order of intensity entirely, something quite literally heartbreaking, said to me, "I really did love him, Aram—oh yes, *really* loved him; he was my first love. . . . When I met your father, he was exactly—I mean he *looked exactly* like Al Pacino in *The Godfather*." And I can still hear the depths of her own bewilderment, and her deep lifelong and still perhaps partly numb hurt, even now inside a long and happy marriage, having had another child who has now just started college. I hear my mother, now no longer young, but this same woman who met my father when she was seventeen years old and looked like a yellow rose with the dew still on it. I hear my mother, now in her fifties, who like my sister Lucy and like me, *grew up* herself, in the end, under the pathological torrent of my father's nervous system—and all of a sudden, sitting outside on a sunny April day in our garden in Bolinas at nine forty-five in the morning, with cocks crowing, and the birds cheeping, I am crying again for the first time since my daughter Strawberry cried the evening of the day we heard my father was dying.

I just called the hospital. It was almost ten o'clock and I wanted to find out how my father had done over the past twenty-four hours. Dr. Jensen-Akula hadn't come in yet, but the nurse told me that my father, who was now awake and alert, was being visited by his cousin Ruben.

She asked if I wanted the call transferred to him, but I declined, now knowing my father's condition and not wanting to risk upsetting him by talking to Ruben.

I can scarcely remember beyond the first few lines—"When have you ever shown any business sense? You're a horse's ass!"—what he said to me on the phone that day after I suggested that I might oversee the repairs on the Malibu place for him.

In any case, it was with these first lines that I knew it was coming. It was as unmistakable as the noise he made of clearing his throat before he spit: another compulsive habit he's had as long as I've known him, something he would do a half a dozen or more times on a walk with me through New York, for instance, and, it occurs to me now, probably something of a parallel habit, in its physical benefits, to his screaming tirades.

But whereas the former habit could be indulged almost at will, the latter required care in selecting a suitable object of abuse. Other than my sister and my mother and me, I know of only his sister Cosette, upon whom he would regularly let out the deeper, one could almost say the visceral levels of his anger, which Cosette, of course, bore mutely and stoically and with her perennial sense of Christian forgiveness.

She, too, was a viable target—what he identified as her stupidity, clumsiness, lack of ability as a cook or housekeeper, or even, I imagine, her affection for me and my wife and family. She was fair game, as it were, because he was for all intents and purposes taking care of her, the income from the Malibu house which he bought in her name being her sole source of income.

"It was like a volcano erupting," my mother said the other night on the phone when I was trying to describe what I now think of as a compulsive, pathological mechanism—and that seems to me perhaps the best image yet. It was, I have no doubt, past a certain point—the first two or three moments—entirely involuntary. "It was his gut," my mother said. "He was like an animal."

I only really remember looking into our living room as epithet piled on epithet, and, still trying somehow—amidst the exclusively aural, but nonetheless powerful, lava flow itself—still trying to hold on to a particular sense I had of my own coming of age, I neither argued with him vehemently, nor hung up, but rather tried in a softer than normal and conciliating voice to talk him out of it.

"Come on, Pop—you don't want to do this . . ."

"What?" he yelled back, louder and madder than ever. "Why you stupid son of a bitch . . ."

It went on and on as I watched the kids moving from their own rooms and into the living room and back again, in the midst of their games in the afternoon light—as Gailyn passed me, on her way from the kitchen to the front garden, carrying some rinse water from doing the dishes to use on the flowers, since we were in the midst of the drought.

As I stood there on the phone that afternoon, I remembered another day, in the winter of early 1969. Gailyn and I had just come back to New York City from a three-month stay in Berkeley, a stay during which I had tried and failed repeatedly to make positive contact with my father, who had been living alternately in Fresno and in San Francisco, but was now himself also in New York.

Then, one afternoon just after we had moved to a friend's apartment—where we lived for the next five or six weeks—I was at my publisher's seeing my editor when the head of the ad department gave me a look as if to say, "I know this must be a screw-up, but . . .," and he told me:

"You know your Dad's in town, and he told Bob Cornfield at Holt that he didn't even *know* where you were, didn't even have your *phone* number. Is that true?"

I probably said something to the effect that I'd just moved to a place a few days ago, asked where my father himself was staying and said I would call him, making light of it as I remember, but underneath infuriated that my father, who had repeatedly refused either to meet or to talk with me when I was in Berkeley, would, for the sake of his own social image, imply to an editor who was both sympathetic to and knowledgeable about my work, that I had somehow cut him off. It made me instantly both very angry and very eager to call him up at his hotel and call his bluff.

And, a couple of hours later, I was standing in the front room of our fourth-floor apartment, as snow fell on Tenth Avenue below, waiting for him to pick up the receiver.

"Hello."

"Pop?"

"Where are you, Aram?"

"I'm staying in an apartment on Tenth Avenue. A friend of mine at Random House told me that you had told Bob Cornfield that you didn't even have my phone number, so I'm calling up to give it to you . . ."

"All right, all right . . ." he said, just getting into gear. "You know a lot of people. Your mother knew a lot of people, too. And you use the telephone. Your mother would make calls to her friends, and you make calls to your friends. You know how to *talk* very well. You're a very good *talker,* and your mother was good at talking. Oh boy. Oh boy."—Here he started screaming.—"Did I get stupid? Did I think I had married a woman who wanted to raise a family, to take care of you and Lucy, her kids? Because you were her kids, you know—that is, she gave *birth* to you. But she's very clever, everybody's clever; you're very clever, too. That's good. You be clever like your mother. Did she give birth to you? No?"

"Pop?"

"You know what you're doing. Good, my boy. Very good. Phone your mother. She likes you. You like her. Phone your mother and see if she will . . ."

"Pop!" This time I had shouted.

He stopped, breathless for a moment.

"Yes?" he said when the moment had passed.

"Go fuck yourself," I said loudly and clearly.

And then, abruptly discharged, he answered me in the language of the military, a language he despises as he despised the army itself—where he spent the first years of his marriage to my mother—but, I suppose, an appropriate form of reply after receiving a command.

"Yes sir," he said swiftly, as if parodying my sudden assumption, at least in his mind, of the role of officer. And he hung up the receiver.

And yet his reply, it occurs to me now, had a peculiar aptness to it. I had simply stopped him in the middle of what, leaving the erupting volcano image for the moment, might alternately be described as a military—in the sense of its being in fact impersonally mechanistic—*attack*. Instead of standing there watching the snow fall outside the windows, as he showered me with psychic bombs and bullets, I had shouted, stopped him and, in effect, asked him impolitely to aim his self-generated arsenal in another direction—his own.

But that was during the sixties and, after a while, I was ashamed of saying "fuck you" to my father, and when he unleashed himself again at me several years later, screaming at me, "You've been running around like a chicken with its head cut off!"—when I had in fact called and asked for his help in putting the down payment on a house in Bolinas, after Gailyn and I and our one-and-a-half-year-old daughter Strawberry had arrived here in the summer of 1972—I didn't make any real reply, and let him go on for the twenty minutes to a half hour that he usually needs to complete his discharge.

And, of course, I did it one last time after offering my help with the Malibu place. I let him get off a complete discharge then, again, and there were a couple of smaller ones in between, usually in letters, which I answered in conciliatory, respectful tones.

Among other things, I reasoned, as I stood in our Bolinas house during that last call, he had grandchildren, three of them now, and, however emotionally unsatisfying and in fact exhausting his semiannual and increasingly whirlwind visits with us had become—he usually brought one or more relatives with him to act as sort of emotional buffer zones—still, I didn't want to deprive either the children or him of their pleasure in seeing one another.

Yesterday there was a report on the news that my father had had a stroke, and we received three calls that were, in effect, responses to this report.

A local woman, Judy Molyneux, who was for a time a close neighbor, called and told Gailyn of the report. Knowing of our estrangement from my father, she said she wasn't sure we would know and felt very sad.

This was at around noon, and she had apparently just heard the report on the radio.

Gailyn said last night that it had been difficult for her to know how to respond to Judy, exactly. She had thanked her warmly for calling.

By nightfall, I had taken two other calls. The first of these, coming late in the afternoon, was from Barry Gifford, a young writer who was my father's editor on his most recent book, *Obituaries*. Barry is also, if distantly, a friend and peer of my own, and I found myself, on what might have been the occasion for at least a brief exchange, uncomfortably reduced to all but mute yes and no replies.

I told him where my father was, and verified that he had fallen into a coma from which he had now revived.

"You mean somebody just found him in his house or something?" Barry asked.

"Yes," I said.

I didn't go on because, if I were to discuss it, I would
want to speak of the cancer itself, and this is apparently
still not known by the media, and in fact, up until a few
days ago, wasn't known by anyone at all other than my
father's doctors and Aram Kevorkian and, presumably,
by Harry Bagdasarian and Ruben Saroyan. It seems to
be against Pop's wishes that anyone be told about it,
even now.

Archie Minasian, one of my father's oldest and closest
friends, who had driven down from Palo Alto to see him
the day they found Pop unconscious, had himself not
been told.

"You still don't see him at all?" Barry asked.

"No," I said, not wanting to go any farther.

"That's too bad . . ." he said with genuine feeling.
"Well—guess we'll send a card or something."

"Yes," I said, by way of a reply.

And that was virtually the end of the call. I didn't want
to speak with Barry in any detail of my estrangement
from my father—for one thing, I was quite certain he
wouldn't want to hear about it. But it was strange and
unnatural not to be able to talk about the situation in any
detail at all, knowing that the word might quite easily and
innocently get around, and then into the papers, causing
Pop further discomfort.

The final caller, in the early evening, was Steve
Saroyan, a man I'd never met, and not, apparently, a
relative.

"I heard about your father, and I wanted to call and
express my condolences."

"Thank you."

"This is just such a . . ." He hesitated, his voice choked
with emotion. ". . . a sad time."

"Yes," I said.

"I just wanted to tell you I know how you must feel."
He seemed on the very verge of tears.

"Thank you," I said.

"All right . . ."

There was a prolonged silence and I said "So long"
and hung up the phone.

Perhaps this is the most difficult thing about my father's dying in the particular way that he has chosen to
die, not wanting to see me or Lucy—that I feel estranged,
in this moment, not only from him, but from the very
reality of his dying itself.

Each day I pick up my pen to write, as if to stave off
what amounts to a deepening dissociation between myself and what is, in fact, happening to my father.

I try to break down what is happening to me, sometimes reaching into the past, to give a name to the deep
restlessness I feel when I am not, in fact, going numb
again. And in naming it, I do, in fact, find some relief
from it.

One of my earliest memories—I could have only been
four or five at the time—is of jumping up and down on
my bed in front of both my mother and my father one
night in a Manhattan apartment before their first divorce,
trying desperately to give them a sense of the feeling I
had inside me which was making it impossible for me to
go to sleep, which they both wanted me to do. I knew
there was a word for my condition, but I couldn't remember what it was, and hence I was doubly frustrated by
what I felt, since I couldn't achieve the sanction of having
it recognized as a known condition for which there was
even, in fact, a specific word. The word I was seeking, of
course, which I believe my father came up with after
more of my jumping up and down and running around,

giving me considerable relief with the label alone, was
"restless."

Now in being kept at this distance from my own father's dying—whatever our previous history—I realize
that I am, once again, and in fact for the final time, in the
palpable grip of his nervous system, tied up by him as I
have, in effect, always been tied up in one way or another.

Each day, as I write and remember, it is as if I am
untying myself. If I can be conscious of my own frustration in the present, my own near agony at times in being
removed this final time from behaving in a normal way
as my father's son—if I can see, if only in writing, the
nature of this strange situation I am now in, for all intents
and purposes emotionally bound and gagged, if I can
give it a name, see its variations throughout the course
of my whole life in my relationship with my father, as
well as in my mother's and my sister's experiences with
him, I hope to go through this final phase of his life
without falling into the alienation of my situation so
deeply that it becomes for me my father's final emotional
coup de grâce.

I am quite literally at war with him now in his last days,
as I have been all along, a strange war in which I am
engaged in trying continually to dispel what is, it now
occurs to me, a sort of emotional bell jar he seems to find
necessary to conjure around me, setting me apart from
the reality of his dying so that I cannot see or hear or
speak to him, and, at the same time, am removed even
from speaking with true candor about the situation with
anyone but my mother and my sister and Gailyn.

Last night Gailyn was saying how strange it is becoming for her—who has, like me, never before experienced

the death of anyone so close—and how thwarted she feels in the midst of this experience.

Maybe we should tell him we'd like to see him again, she suggested.

I felt immediately dubious at best about doing this, without quite knowing why.

My father is dying. Then he goes into a coma, bringing him presumably right to the doors of death. People have been known to go through total transformations after such an experience, Gailyn said, and maybe he has, and now wants to see me, or the kids, but is too proud to say so.

Then it occurred to me that I could call Dr. Jensen-Akula this morning and tell him that I would like to see my father and that if he would like to see me, I will drive down, and ask the doctor to give this message to Pop, and to call me back with Pop's reply.

But then I realized that I had just been writing about an incident which had its more immediate counterpart in Pop's conversation with Aram Kevorkian, in which he ended up saying that Lucy might spend an hour or so a day with him if she were in Fresno. I had just been writing of my father's behavior in New York in 1969, when he had, simply for the sake of his own emotional convenience at the moment, committed himself to a bald-faced social lie—implying he wanted to see me, didn't even know where I was, etc. This is a form of self-serving expediency in which he doesn't consider the cost: Lucy packing her bags and driving up to see him after hearing from Aram Kevorkian; my own almost immediate telephone call to him after talking with the ad manager at my publisher's—a visit and a call, respectively, he was in no sense ready, willing, or able to accept.

This brings me to a dimension of my father's character for which I know I have so deep a distrust, because I can see my distrust in the course of my own life choices, completely independent of him, that it amounts to—even including an ambivalent element in me—the deepest personal loathing. He is an emotional grandstander. He plays to the gallery. He is, in his own person, very like one of his own sentimental favorites: the whore with the heart of gold—which is, after all, in the deepest sense, an emotional impossibility.

Even on what may be his deathbed at the Veterans Administration Hospital in Fresno, his doctor having posed the question of my visit, I wouldn't it put it past him to answer whatever he senses might most enhance his own image, socially, at that moment, as I believe he did with Aram Kevorkian regarding the visit from his daughter.

And it was Lucy, of course, who picked up the tab.

My father's fame itself has entrenched, to the degree of institutionalizing it, this pattern of both public and self deception. It has made it possible for him to remain unknown not only to his public, that is, but also—by giving him the easy out of the adulation, and, in the case of the Armenians, the outright coddling of their unquestioning and in fact blind acceptance—to remain, in essence, unknown to himself as well.

William Saroyan is, after all, quite simply one of the most lovable father figures of American letters. It is the *family* he speaks of so poignantly in his best-loved books: *My Name Is Aram,* a selection of stories which are essentially a fictionalized account of his own Fresno boyhood that was published when he was thirty; and *The Human Comedy,* the most novelistic of his novels, which was, significantly, first written as a screenplay (for which he won the Academy Award for the Best Original Screenplay of 1943) just before he met my mother, and which portrays an American family during World War II, but is in essence, like *My Name Is Aram,* a fictionalized—and, of course, rather idealized—memoir of his own boyhood in the days of World War I.

These books are, quite simply, about the joys and sorrows of family life, and the people who know this work, and love it, must find it more or less in the dimension of the incredible that William Saroyan, with all the sweetness to be found in these books, high-school reading list favorites for the past twenty-five years, wouldn't himself be, in fact, one of the most wonderful and understanding fathers of all time.

And all of this, of course, has made for a significant variety of tensions in my own life. In the first place, the books were written when my father was still single, before he tried, and in fact did not succeed at, becoming a family man himself.

Sons Come & Go, Mothers Hang In Forever, the curious title of one of his later, more sober-voiced memoirs, comes to mind now—specifically, the sudden shift of gender, as well as generation, between the two sides of the title separated by the comma.

Sons come and go, but fathers—no, *mothers . . .* hang in forever. For his own father, Armenak, was gone at thirty-five.

But the "mothers" in the title is used in its vernacular, street slang sense—short for mother-fuckers. This is the sense, at least, that is substantiated by the book itself, which includes portraits of several of these prominent "mothers," including L. B. Mayer, who bought the screenplay of *The Human Comedy* in a deal in which my father has always felt he was cheated.

But such a "mother" hangs in forever, as opposed to a son. And this, in turn, makes me think of my father's Uncle Aram (after whom I believe that I was named, at least in a certain sense, although my father claims that Aram is simply his favorite name for a man) and of Aram's son, my father's cousin Chesley, the failed writer, who died in his forties in a manner that might be construed as a suicide.

Uncle Aram, the younger brother of my father's mother, Takoohi, was, after the death of Armenak, quite simply the nearest at hand and quite certainly the most impressive male role model in the family orbit once my father got back from the orphanage.

The most vivid memory I have of this man is of a visit my father and I believe Archie Minasian once paid him at an apartment he had in San Francisco while he was briefly between his first and second marriages, a visit on which I tagged along, but couldn't actually participate in much, since the talk was almost entirely in Armenian. I believe I was still a teenager at the time.

I remember Uncle Aram, a barrel-chested man then in his sixties, standing in the middle of the room dressed only in boxer shorts—it was an overcast but muggy day outside—while my father and Archie and I sat on the sofa against the wall, watching Aram tell one story after another in a voice that usually reached a loud roar as the story ended, causing both my father and Archie to collapse with helpless laughter, a laughter at which I, in turn, would laugh, in lieu of actually understanding the story. And Aram would now wait, politely, with a little grin on his face, as my father and Archie gradually got hold of themselves, pulled themselves together, and then, scarcely letting the pause go long enough for either of them to get a word in edgewise, he would begin another story.

He is a family legend, still alive and now in his eighties.

My father told me that it was Aram who had brought Takoohi and Cosette and Zabelle and Henry—as well as his own and Takoohi's mother, Lucy, a woman said to be very wise—over on the boat to America to join Armenak; that at only twelve years of age, Aram had taken care of them during this passage.

It was said, in fact, that Aram had made a lot of money during this passage by mastering a gambling game that was current among the émigrés.

Two men, each holding an egg, would knock eggs together and the man whose egg broke first lost. Aram had discovered that by boiling his egg while keeping it in a position where the substance of the egg was weighted in the egg's apex, and then leading with the apex, knocking with it, during the game, he would consistently win.

So, at twelve, he was already uniquely gifted with street smarts—in vivid contrast with my father's father, Armenak, a dreamer who was remembered by his friends and family members very affectionately, but with perhaps just a shadow of scorn as well, as someone almost literally "too good for this world." And, in fact, my father might be seen as a curious amalgam of his two father figures: his own father, Armenak, who was, essentially, a poet; and his uncle, Aram, who was the embodiment of the successful American immigrant, having become a celebrated criminal lawyer in Fresno in his thirties.

He was a fiery, dramatic, impatient man who both thwarted my father's own deepest desires—literally trying to kick him out of the house after he had quit his job in order to become a writer—and, almost at one and the same time, deeply delighted him. (Or did this delight come only in the retrospect provided by my father's literary success?) There was such a *physical* sense of confidence and authority about the man; he was, in his very being itself, like a work of art: in the sly and shrewd composure with which he went about his life and business; and in the sudden wild comic invention of which, on the spur of the moment, he was capable.

Once, after my father and mother had gotten married and they were considering buying a house with acreage for a small vineyard, my father went to look at a certain property in Fresno, and Uncle Aram came along.

It was a sweltering day, especially so in the house itself, and my father made some comment to this effect, to which the real-estate agent, most likely not to be daunted from his sales pitch, pointed out that the house had a phone.

"What?!" Uncle Aram roared at the man. "The phone's going to cool him off?!"

My father loved this capacity for outrage, combined with simple common sense, that he found embodied in Aram: when he told this story of his uncle, which I heard him repeat with the same delight again and again, it was as if he were celebrating the male life-force itself. Certainly, anyone at all, my father would suggest, and he himself as quickly as anyone else, could find failings in Aram, could point, self-righteously, to his overweening pride, his sheer obtuseness with regard to my father's own ambitions, etc.—but, in the end, my father seemed to want to have it, the man couldn't really be faulted, couldn't really be justly criticized. In the midst of his own rambunctious nonstop involvements and declarations, he himself, of course, wouldn't have time for these petty qualifications in the first place. He had too much to *do* to put up with these finer points. He was, quintessentially and unimpeachably, simply a *man:* he was a provider; he was an American success.

*   *   *

Whereas Armenak, my father's actual father, of whom he had in fact almost no memories, was himself the bleakest sort of failure imaginable: a failure as a preacher, a failure as a poet, a failure as a husband and a father. And what was it that sealed this failure, and made it final and irrevocable?

Armenak died before my father was scarcely at the age of consciousness, and hence he deprived my father of even a genuinely conscious recognition of his death.

At this moment, I realize I am speaking of something I felt for the first time the other night as I moved from the living-room table, carrying some dinner dishes to the kitchen sink amidst the clutter and noise of the after-dinner hour. The kids were in the last phase of their day's activity—Armenak playing with blocks on the floor; Strawberry doing her homework at her desk in her room; Cream, in fact, falling asleep, curled up in her yellow flannel nightgown on the living-room sofa—when suddenly it came to me that as my father dies, my own link in the mortal chain, in a certain sense, opens, hooking, as it were, into oblivion. Whereas *before* he dies, it is his link that opens into it, not mine. He is still in front of me in a line of succession, as my children are behind me:

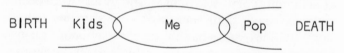

—whereas when my father dies, it will be more like, though not entirely (since my mother is still alive), this:

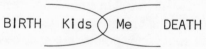

An extended family is, in this sense, like a kind of cozy, mortal haven during the middle of one's life, that time when one is most specifically concerned with the business of the world.

And I simultaneously realized that what had happened to my father when Armenak died before my father was quite three years old, and his mother virtually disappeared as well, is that his just barely begun mortal link was abruptly and finally truncated, so that instead of existing at the birth end of the chain, his link hooked into the abyss at *both* ends:

BIRTH   Pop at 3   DEATH

—causing him, I surmise, to go into an involuntary, and in fact prerational freeze, which I believe he is still in at this very moment, sixty-nine years later, and in fact now about to die.

And it occurs to me that this might be seen as the primary reason it has been impossible for my father from the very beginning to acknowledge either Lucy or me as his children in any but the most baffling and frustrating manner imaginable—since he himself was cut off from any personal sense of mortal succession in fact before the age of reason. That is, his own link hooked up at the very moment of the dawning of his rational consciousness not with father, or mother—but with Death itself. And he would be frozen in this posture, quite literally without a link at either end of his mortal chain, for the rest of his life.

And my sister and I, in turn, would never be able to link up with him naturally, as a part of his and our own mortal cycle. Instead, our situation would look more like this:

—and in between ourselves and our father, there existed what was either poisonous, as when he erupted from his own momentarily unfreezing, death-marked depths, or, perhaps even more disorienting, because even more deeply baffling, there existed a kind of invisible shield between us, as if Lucy and I both existed in that emotional bell jar I have spoken of in relation to him, so that instead of having our emotions toward him accepted and shared by him, we would reach out only to find ourselves strangely thwarted, as if by some invisible glass, our own feelings toward him sealed off in a way not unlike, to come full circle in the succession of images, the sealed Mason jar full of money.

One of my earliest memories of my father goes back to the house we lived in on Taravel Street in San Francisco when I was three years old.

One evening, as he sat at the far end of the living room, I held my thumb and index finger together to make a circle, and then touched this circle to different objects in the room, as well as to parts of the air itself; and each time I brought the circle to rest somewhere, I would say, "There's an angel here."

"There's an angel here," I would say, touching the corner of a table.

"And there's an angel here," I would say, touching the air next to the table.

"And there's an angel here," I would say, bringing my hand to a cigarette box on the table.

I remember my father looking at me from the far end of the room and remaining absolutely mute, so that I abandoned any notions of approaching him physically, in what was, after all, a magical mood not unfamiliar in children.

There was a sort of faint smile on his face, but a smile that seemed to me to contain some ambivalence toward me, not quite censuring, but at the same time a far cry from warmly affectionate.

And this forced me back upon myself—even at that very moment, at three years old, I felt suddenly as though I were *performing* before my father rather than simply sharing something I was feeling with him, and I even began to wonder whether my performance wasn't altogether too grandiose and precious, as if I were trying to upstage what was after all his superior adult wisdom.

What I am trying to characterize here is the severe self-consciousness that is brought on by living inside a situation in which one feels emotionally thwarted. It becomes increasingly difficult to accept one's own emotional impulses. One begins to lower the invisible shield on one's own emotional reality.

"In sympathy lies contagion," Gide tells us; and in the child that I was, there was only the most natural sense of acceptance and love for my father. If he looked at me funny, *I* looked at me funny, too.

In my mother's case, another dimension she had to contend with was his fame—which, as I say, because he could always retreat to the adoration of his admirers, functioned as a shield between my father and any genuine self-knowledge.

And this leads me back to Uncle Aram, who my father almost defensively continued to insist was a great man, even as certain dimensions of Aram's life seemed to cast an unfavorable light back at him.

His son Chesley, for instance, who was a young man beloved by almost all of the members of his extended family, a special one, another poet of the Saroyan clan.

And Chesley, as I myself was later to do, got married early, to a woman named Amie, and they started a family. During the war, the story goes, while living in Paris and trying to become a writer, he was the novelist Malcolm Lowry's drinking buddy and used to make sure that Lowry, an entrenched alcoholic, got home safely each night.

My father, in Europe himself, after his first divorce from my mother, saw Chesley during this period, and Chesley gave his famous cousin one of his fledgling literary efforts for his opinion. Over the years, my father told me of his response to Chesley's effort several times, as if to impart the lesson to me as well: "Chesley," he told the aspiring writer, "clean your typewriter."

But what was Chesley's story like, I would ask Pop. Here he became rather vague, and more compassionate: It was about Chesley's life at the time—what else *would* it be about? About confused young people trying to make a life—and it was interesting, in its way, but it was still confused in the writing. Good earnest apprentice work.

But his own comment about Chesley's typewriter needing to be cleaned was what had stuck in my father's mind. And I can't help but wonder if it wasn't what stuck in Chesley's mind as well. In its practical, utilitarian emphasis it is the sort of comment that might have reminded Chesley of his father Aram; and I can't help but think that my father failed Chesley here in what was, after all, a rather brave act of self-exposure to his older cousin Bill, a world-famous writer.

Then something happened. How and why I have no way of knowing, but it became clear that something was seriously wrong with Chesley. His marriage broke up, and it was said that he was in and out of sanatariums, much to his father Aram's deep chagrin.

I met Chesley when I was around twenty and he was perhaps my age now, if not a little older. He looked older still. Easily forty-five or so. He was balding, and there was a strange, recessive quality about him.

I had come across the country on the spur of the moment—having run into someone in New York who was just about to drive to L.A. From there I made my way by Greyhound up to San Francisco and my father.

My father then decided to visit Fresno with me—he was staying in Cosette's house, before he had bought his Fresno houses. We drove down there one morning, and, as he liked to do, ended up getting a kind of informal and mobile party going as we went around to various relatives' houses: they would offer food and drink before we moved on again—our erstwhile hosts now joining us themselves as often as not—to the house of another relative.

At some point that day, we all had a big barbeque on the patio of one relative's ranch house, and there was lots of boisterous laughter, lots of food and drink—a family occasion, warm if never really intimate—and it was here that I remember seeing Chesley.

He was a trim man, and there was something attractive about him, something that set him apart from the others. It was as if, singularly, he had known the love of a woman who had been his equal—amidst the usually extreme chauvinism of the Armenian patriarchy—and however it had turned out, he had been marked by it, quieted, so that it was impossible for him to be too carried away with the family festivities of the day. Not that he didn't enjoy them, only that you sensed another, deeper dimension to him that could not release itself in terms of the Armenian, mostly male tribe we were now all of us inside and celebrating.

*   *   *

Later that afternoon, driving somewhere, Chesley and I got into a brief argument. I was, in my way, the twenty-year-old upstart on the literary horizon in the family. Chesley himself, deeply loved by everyone as he was, had been by now determined a failure. It was said that he spent his days playing Ping-Pong with firemen between their calls, since he happened to live above a firehouse.

Earlier, he had tried his hand at being a shoe salesman. Uncle Aram, my father told me, had been deeply hurt that his eldest son would end up with this sort of lowly employment, and Pop himself seemed to identify with Aram's disappointment far more readily than with Chesley's pain.

He was apparently quite deeply touched by the pathos of his rich and powerful uncle finding his son not equal to any better job. Pop liked to imitate Aram's overzealous and hence obviously wounded defense of Chesley, his loud declaration at the time that "Chesley is the best goddamned shoe salesman in the world!"

A great man, the message to me was, disappointed by his son.

My father also liked to imitate Aram's more or less helpless insistence on certain personal standards, even in the face of Chesley's crack-up. In fact, I believe this story originated with Chesley himself, who told it to Pop, I imagine, as a kind of character capsule of his father, Uncle Aram. When Aram was seeing Chesley onto a bus that would take him to the asylum, he could not restrain himself, as Chesley waited to board the bus, from whispering urgently into his ear: "Chesley, stand up straight!"

But, as I say, when my father told this story or the one about Chesley being the best shoe salesman in the world, there was less a sense that he felt sorrow and compassion for Chesley, than that he continued to be startled into deeper and deeper levels of admiration for Uncle Aram, as cruel as he might have been to Chesley. He seemed quite literally to admire the steadfastness of Uncle Aram's personal standards.

How amazing, after all, that this man could still be concerned about his son's *posture* when Chesley's mind had cracked!

Amazing indeed, and, in my father's mind, deeply moving.

But I was, as I say, the upstart writer, my father's son, and I was out to prove that I knew more than anybody around, including Pop, about what *really* went on in literature. And I was a real smart guy in those days. I figured out where the action was and I went for it, and I had certainly left the likes of Chesley way, way behind.

Chesley liked Robert Burns's "My luve is like a red, red rose . . ."

I replied something to the effect that this was sentimental poetry, and was not, in any case, truly modern—there had been, since Burns, tremendous *progress* made in poetry.

I must have sounded like a literary Uncle Aram. And the poor man, when I turned around to look at him from the front seat of my father's car, let out a kind of inaudible, and yet, to me, just visible spasm of absolute madness —and, clever boy that I was, I backed off with the sudden knowledge that I'd better watch myself because Chesley was, after all, actually crazy.

The only regret that I have in all this is that over the next ten or fifteen years, it became increasingly clear to me that Chesley was, indeed, right about Robert Burns and his "My luve is like a red, red rose . . ." And that I was a twenty-year-old horse's ass.

*   *   *

The following year, ensconced in my first apartment in New York City, a one-room studio on East Forty-fifth Street, I was startled one morning to open a package in my mail and find a thin light-blue hardbound volume, bearing my own name—and I was now, after all, a published poet—but with the unexpected and in fact absolutely uncharacteristic title *Cheated Death by Inches.*

My friends among the poets of the New York School were not above an occasional elaborate joke of this order, but it was unlikely that they had the money to produce a hardcover, and in fact a leather-bound volume.

After further inspection, I realized that this book was the product of my father's Uncle Aram, sent to me, perhaps, because I was now a writer myself.

At twenty pages or so, it was an amazing volume. Subtitled *The Authentic Story of My Automobile Accident,* and graced with an epigraph from Knute Rockne— "When the going gets tough, the tough get going"—it told the story, in a prose style that might be characterized as high class immigrant, of how Uncle Aram had gone off a cliff in his car, broken virtually every bone in his body, had had his soul pass down into hell and seen the devil with his tail and a pitchfork, and then gone up into heaven where a lot of little white fluffy angels whispered in his ear, and had, after all this, lived to tell about it.

Cheated Death by Inches—the big guy had chalked up another victory, this time against the heaviest of all the heavyweights, Death itself. Was the man, in fact, not outright immortal?

It occurred to me that putting this book into circulation among my poet friends as my own work might be considered something in the nature of a surrealist coup, but I somehow never quite did anything with the idea.

*   *   *

Now here is the strange part, and the part that still echoes in me. Several years after Uncle Aram's accident, his son Chesley, perhaps less entirely accidentally, had a very similar car crash, driving off a cliff himself, and when his car came to rest, finally, it caught fire, and Chesley was burned, alive or already dead, in the wreck.

The parallel in the two accidents confounds and fascinates me. It is almost as if Chesley were saying to his father, "No, Pop, you got it all wrong, *this* is the way you do it—when you go off a cliff like that, you're supposed to *die,* not live." It is almost as if Chesley's death in this manner is a kind of final, poignant commentary on his father's continuing life, pointing to its missing element, and in fact to a source of pride to Uncle Aram himself: his refusal, both literally and figuratively, to die; his refusal, that is, to admit a dimension of surrender into his experience in any form. It is almost as if Chesley, in this final act of his brief life, were trying to teach his already aged father Aram how to surrender, how to die.

Sons Come & Go, Mothers Hang In Forever.

This morning, I decided, finally, to call Dr. Jibelian, instead of Dr. Jensen-Akula at the hospital, reasoning that Pop had already told Dr. Jibelian that he didn't want to see me, so that he would be less inclined to lie for the sake of appearances. The doctor agreed to ask him if he would like a visit from any of us when he saw him later in the afternoon.

This past Thursday there was a short item, with a Fresno dateline, in the *San Francisco Chronicle* entitled "William Saroyan Stable After Having a Stroke," which was the gist of the item itself. Yesterday, however, there was a longer follow-up article in the *Chronicle* that was both surprising and mysterious to me. This article, from the Associated Press, bore the headline "Doctor Says Saroyan Has Cancer, Didn't Have Stroke," and, under a Fresno dateline, read as follows:

> Author William Saroyan yesterday was reported ill with cancer at a hospital and did not suffer a stroke as was reported earlier this week, a physician reported. Saroyan was reported as "alert and comfortable."
>
> Saroyan, 72, whose works include "The Time of Your Life" and "The Human Comedy," was hospitalized Monday after being found unconscious at his home.
>
> Saroyan telephoned the Associated Press bureau here last week and reported he has cancer of the liver, heart, kidneys and bones.
>
> Dr. Robert Aduan of the Veterans Administration Medical Center said cancer "contributed to his hospitalization, but he is not receiving any treatment for that at this time."
>
> A cancer specialist was among the physicians consulting on Saroyan's case, Aduan said.
>
> "He's very alert and comfortable this morning,"

Aduan said. "I think he will leave the hospital, but I can't say when."

Aduan discounted earlier reports that Saroyan suffered a stroke.

"I don't think we have any evidence he has had a stroke," the doctor said.

The first surprise, of course, was that word of the cancer had somehow gotten to the media. I immediately felt guilty now for clamming up on the subject of Pop's illness with Barry Gifford, and with the writer Nona Balakian, who called the next day. The first time I read the article, in fact, I skimmed it and more or less took the third paragraph, regarding my father phoning the Associated Press office in Fresno *last week* and telling them he had cancer, as some sort of misprint.

It was only after Gailyn read the story and called my attention to this part that I read it again, more baffled than ever. After all these months of secrecy, perhaps even years of it, why would he do such a thing?

Then, this afternoon, Lucy phoned and we had a long talk. She is down again. The other night, returning to her apartment after an evening with friends, she felt terribly alone, suddenly, and ended up crying—and continued crying, unable to stop herself, so that she became frightened that her crying might literally go on forever.

"I was really scared, Ar, you know? I mean I really thought that it was never going to end."

She was only able to stop, at last, after an hour and a half. I tried to take a positive view of it, telling her that I thought she was now letting her grief pass through her, etc.

We also discussed the most recent news item on Pop, which had also appeared in the L.A. papers. I questioned that Pop himself would have actually called the Associated Press and broken the story of his own illness last week. But Lucy was convinced that he had.

"One of the things that he really harped on with me, Ar, was how I exploit famous people. 'I'm not gonna name names, but I know all about it,' he said."

Lucy has, in fact, dated several famous actors, if that can be considered exploitation, as well as worked recently in a film with her famous stepfather, Walter Matthau, for which she later did a promotional tour.

"I'm sure he phoned the Associated Press the minute he kicked me out, so that he would beat me to the press conference he figured I was going to set up right away to announce that my father was dying. He did it, Ar. I know he did it. Nobody else would say that about cancer of the heart."

"Right," I said. "There is no such thing."

"Right—or only Pop knows about it . . . He did it."

After I had talked with Lucy, Gailyn and I discussed the news story again, and she wondered why the Associated Press didn't print the story when they first got it. It occurred to me that until the story of the stroke appeared, they might have considered it a crank call.

Someone calls up, out of the blue, and says: "This is William Saroyan. I'm calling to tell you that I have cancer of the liver, heart, kidneys and bones."

What does a reporter make of such a phone call? And, even if he suspects that it might, in fact, *be* William Saroyan, how does he write it up, and under what title? "Telephone Call from William Saroyan"—? But once the article appeared regarding the stroke, maybe the reporter remembered the phone call again, did a bit of checking, and came up with the new story.

At least Pop—clever as a fox with cancer of the heart —beat Lucy to it.

APRIL 27, 1981 / Monday, 4:00 A.M.

At a certain point, the current breaks, the sustained meditation of this past week or so falters, I find myself somehow irresolute in my own desire to go on. I take a day or two off. Gailyn, after resting up this past winter, suddenly begins to paint again—two new paintings in two days, full of the actual light of our own lives, the flowers in the window, the curtains and the books . . .

My father remains in his bed at the hospital, though it is said he is soon to return to his home. Yesterday, Sunday, I called my Aunt Cosette, with whom I haven't spoken in several months, having gradually abandoned my habit of phoning her every Sunday after turning away from my father. It became clear to me that he kept tabs on us through his sister, and I wanted the break as clean and clear as possible. And Cosette, poor woman, couldn't help but be his champion.

These four children—though the other sister, Zabelle, died several years ago now, also of cancer—are, perhaps, the true family they all found and held on to through life. They are guardians of one another, helplessly protesting my father's virtue to me over the years. (I am speaking of Cosette and Henry, for the most part, since Zabe, as she was known, had a family of four children and countless grandchildren of her own, which kept her absorbed and, for the most part, beyond my own immediate orbit.) I understand this in them and cannot, in the end, protest it. It seems to me, in its own way, so admirable.

My father used to like to tell the story of his older brother interceding on his behalf, when he was a small boy being bullied by an older boy. Henry jumped into the fray and swiftly delivered a blow, stopping the other boy dead in his tracks, and also eliciting a spontaneous testimonial from the boy, as he held his jaw in wonder.

"Henry," my delighted father would imitate the other boy saying, "you've got a hand like a rock!"

When Henry, a dapper and clear-voiced man at the age of seventy-six, the retired chief accountant with ABC's San Francisco office, talked with me on the telephone in the heat of last week's crisis, there couldn't help but be a certain dimension of estrangement between us. Why hadn't I made it up with Pop long ago? To Henry, after all, it was a simple matter.

"You're his son, he's your father—'Hi, son'; 'Hi, Pop' —you sit down, you talk."

And hearing this from him on the phone was as salutary, in its way, as seeing my daughter Strawberry's simple human grief at the imminent death of her grandfather.

The world turns, after all, by the same powers that these simple and beautiful emotions make evidence of. My father's estrangement from the family he founded may be a hard, rocklike fact in the midst of the otherwise for the most part fluid emotional currents of his family at large. But those currents nevertheless flow around him, embracing him, wetting him down even in the lonely and bitter stand he has taken through the years. Perhaps to his brother, sister, and countless cousins, after all, this stand is not altogether without some poignant majesty of its own. These are, quite simply, his people, his own very blood. They will put up with him whatever he does, they will see him through.

It is that simple—and beautiful.

And, of course, they are all very proud of him, too. He is their truest American success.

It is difficult for me here not to accept this outright, in loving admiration of both my aunt and my uncle, but I would be less than honest if I let it go quite so simply. For my father's success as a writer had an effect on his immediate family, as on the larger family of the Armenian race as a whole, of removing him almost entirely from the realm of mortal foibles and failings, of rendering him—for the pride that his success brought to these two groups, one small and the other large—an all-but-Godlike example of unassailable perfection. And this, of course, blighted his life as surely as his early experience blighted it.

Cosette sounded well on the phone yesterday. She hadn't been told of my father's illness until "the stroke," which came as a severe shock to her.

"The first two nights after I heard, honey," she told me, "I couldn't sleep at all, and I was sitting up in bed crying—just thinking of him like that, unconscious, in the hospital."

Her kindness and goodwill toward my father, in the face of abuses I have already discussed, is truly remarkable to me. But even more remarkable was the strange youthfulness and openness in her voice yesterday—as if her Christian spirit has in fact given her something that surpasses anything that could come out of a stricter emotional bookkeeping. She is, quite simply, at eighty-two, still young.

She told me she had received a call from Harry Bagdasarian before I called, and that Harry had just called to let her know what had been happening.

"He says Bill wants to go home, but he can't yet, he

has to stay for a while, because he's too weak. He wouldn't be able to walk. But he says he's Bill again. He's lying in bed, but he's ordering all his cousins around, telling them what to do . . ."

And here she laughs, sweetly and sincerely and very much like a young girl, at this phenomenon she has known, in fact, all his natural life, because she herself was already ten years old when he was born—her brother, Bill.

And still this whole experience for me is like one long moment of dissociation. I follow the thought patterns— my own interior thought patterns—almost as if they are another person's. Thoughts of all kinds—not just those dwelling on my father. His refusal to see me is also a refusal to allow his death to be real to me. My father is dying and I can scarcely feel it—but the air is charged with a kind of savage discontinuity: words and feelings separate, and assume an independent, depersonalized mobility.

Lucy said on the phone the other day that when she got into her car after my father had kicked her out of the house, she was suddenly driving without knowing where the car ended and she began, not knowing if she was the windshield, or her hand on the steering wheel.

One day when I was eight years old, after my parents had divorced for the second time, and my mother had taken Lucy and me out of the small mansion on North Rodeo Drive in Beverly Hills that we had all lived in during the second marriage, and moved us into a one-bedroom apartment on the corner of Olympic Boulevard and McCarty Drive—one day I kneeled down on the sidewalk and held the front of my bike up off the ground, so that I could spin the front wheel.

When I gave the wheel a spin, one side of it was directly in front of me. I think I had seen someone else do this, and I wanted to watch the spokes disappear as the wheel spun. Suddenly, as the spokes before me now disappeared, all the neighborhood noises—the traffic off the boulevard, the dull roar of all urban neighborhoods, a pedestrian walking by, a shout some distance away, "HEY!"—every noise, and all at once, in a whole seamless aural tapestry, was invaded by another sound pattern. It was as if suddenly all sound became uniformly wrinkled, with wrinkles within wrinkles, and this pattern seemed to grow progressively denser. Were it to go much farther, I would lose any sense of the actual noises and become submerged in the advance of these sonic waves, which would eventually embrace the whole of my own nervous system in its advance so that all of me, too, would become a part of this pattern—and I would be mad.

I stopped the wheel. And stood up in the sunny day, as if to remove myself out of the hypnotic advancing spell of the intricate waves of sound. The sound seemed to contain an underlying voice that was something like a continuous whispering, the very words themselves wrinkled beyond recognition. Yet what they contained, which I could understand from their underlying "tone," was mockery. As if all that I heard was a whispering behind my back, the whole world whispering some mockery of me.

During this period of my life, this sound pattern would advance periodically—and then would recede again. It never became so serious that it threatened to actually take over. I could even feel it, occasionally, years later.

And it had what seems to me now to have been a sort of visual counterpart, which I believe I also experienced for the first time during this period, and which would also recur every so often years later: I wake up in my own room, but everything in it, as well as the arrangement of the furniture, and even the very character of the light, seems to me ineluctably and infuriatingly "wrong." The sensation would gradually pass as I became fully awake.

The way my father is dying is his final act of mental and psychological cruelty to Lucy and me. He simply refuses to admit our reality as his son and daughter as he goes through his last moments of life.

This is, I believe, a last dance into the nether depths of his violence at us. It is unspeakably frustrating to me to go through it day by day.

Today the scrapbook was returned to us in the envelope I sent it in to Pop. The short note I had attached to the first page in the scrapbook was also returned. It reads, in its entirety, "4/17/81 . . . Dear Pop, Here's our most recent scrapbook . . . All our love, Aram & Gailyn & the kids."

The only indication that my father received it at all is on the envelope, the large Jiffy bag I sent it in and in which he returned it. It reads, in his hand, on the right side just under the postage, in the black ink of a fountain pen: "Sunday 1150 AM/April 19 1981." And slightly under this, in larger handwriting and underlined: "Great Easter Gift."

On the left side of the Jiffy bag, at about parallel height, it says, in larger handwriting, also my father's, and written with a black Flair pen, "Ruben/Return to Aram/ regular mail."

All of the above, on both sides of the envelope, has been crossed out—presumably by Ruben Saroyan, who apparently addressed the Jiffy bag to me, or by somebody at the post office—along with the "Special Delivery" stamped three times on the bag when I originally mailed it.

I know I'm supposed to feel grateful, and I did in fact feel a lump in my throat when I picked up the package at the post office this afternoon, with Armenak along. On our way back to the car he said, "I think Grandpa Bill liked the scrapbook. I think he did."

"Yes, I think he did," I answered, smiling at him.

Yes, I should be grateful, but it is somehow not quite possible for me. The best I can do is to go on waiting out this final red infantry action on my own psyche, his absolute refusal to accept me sustained right through the final hours of his life, when I will not and cannot nail him on it, as I nailed him when I turned away three and a half years ago, nailed him in his own game, ignoring him back, as he essentially ignored me.

But I have no choice now. I have broken my own course—for the sake of my conscience; for the sake of my children—but he will keep to his. The only way I can hold my own now is by writing it down day by day until the terrible game is over at last.

It is almost as if my father's lifelong condition of emotional exile is being passed on to me each day in this long final episode of his life.

It is a last reprisal of all that has gone before and I find myself alternately murderously angry and helplessly fascinated to notice the very depths to which his condition reaches me, as well as remembering earlier moments in my life when I became seized by the dissociation in ways that remain vivid.

My own daily condition is now in fact like a kind of museum of his emotional effects, by which I may in turn read the pattern of my whole life. Last night Gailyn and I lay in bed, discussing this.

"But why don't you just *feel* it, the emotion, instead of all this intellectualizing."

"I feel it," I said. "But all it is, is hatred."

"Good. Let it come through. Punch a pillow or something."

I did, in fact, punch a pillow a week or so ago for a while. Actually, just throwing punches at the air, in lieu of a punching bag, turned out to be more satisfying.

"But," I tried to explain, "this is something that's been going on for thirty-seven years with me. I'm just beginning to realize the depths it reaches down into."

"That's true," she answered. "It's different for me, I guess. I haven't known him, really. But I feel it, still. What depths?"

"A lot of stuff. I'm just feeling him every day now in the pit of my stomach, something way down there now, and if I can notice it, the feeling, and *name* it, that defuses it somewhat."

"But what depths specifically?"

"I couldn't learn to read. When I did learn how, I could read a passage without understanding it at all, over and over again. I could listen to someone speaking and hear their words but not what they were saying."

As I wrote yesterday, I also experienced hypnogogic hallucinations, where one element, in this instance sound, threatens to take over the sensorium, causing an imbalance that could lead to madness itself.

All of this is what is going on, to one extent or another, again now. My father has refused to accept me emotionally all my life and this has had a profound impact on that life, encompassing in me, at times, the very character of perception itself.

After her second divorce from my father, my mother, too, found it increasingly hard to focus her attention on Lucy or me—or, I imagine, on anyone or anything at all. She seemed to live for several years in a state of sustained distraction.

Her emotional currents, like my own and like my sister's, had simply been short-circuited to the degree that her entire sensorium was seemingly dismantled. I mean by this something very literal, at least in my own case.

I mean that my eyes, ears, nose, sense of touch and taste—all my senses—were at times out of precise harmony, the *physically* synchronized harmony that is supported and ultimately enforced by a favorable emotional environment.

My father's inability to accept emotion, either in himself or from others, created an environment that involved a sort of continual short circuit—and this in turn, I believe, led to severe forms of sensory deprivation in the members of his own immediate family.

When the crisis was most severe in my life, at eight years old, after the second divorce, an angel appeared.

Her name was Martha Goetz, she was a close friend of my mother's, and for some reason she took an interest in me.

Martha was a woman of around thirty, blond and of a delicate, thin-featured beauty. She spoke with a peculiar rhythm that to me at eight sounded slightly sarcastic—a waspish tone—and, when I first began to get to know her, I was afraid she would find me stupid.

But if this happened, she never in fact let on.

In the midst of those chaotic and unhappy days—I remember my mother trying to learn from Martha how to drive a car one hot Los Angeles afternoon; trying for about a quarter of an hour to get into a parking space— Martha began to take me to what were, at that time in Los Angeles, the minor-league local baseball games.

At the time I was flunking the third grade at a Catholic school a few blocks from where we lived, where Lucy and I had been enrolled. I was barely able to read anything at all, let alone catechism. I was frequently told by the nun who was my teacher to stay in the classroom during recess, and kneel at my desk and say one hundred Hail Marys. The strange fact was, I found myself actually praying.

Perhaps Martha herself was the answer to those prayers. For while in school I was perilously close to giving myself up for a hopeless ignoramus, one who would never be able to learn and master the skills by which other people made their way in the world, Martha would take me to a night game—the Hollywood Stars versus the Los Angeles Angels—and, sitting in her box near the first-base line, she would patiently instruct me on how to keep a box score, and she even managed to give me the sense that I was picking it up quite easily and smoothly —so that, while I did in fact flunk the year at the Catholic school (the next school I went to allowed me to advance to my proper grade), I didn't lose the sense that I could learn, which would have made my life amount to a kind of living death.

Martha seemed to find me pleasant company. Here she was, a beautiful married Beverly Hills woman with a daughter, Townsend, a few years older than I, and for some reason she went out of her way to be kind to me. And, I have no doubt of it, she saved my very life.

Yesterday evening I decided to go to see my father. I had talked with Dr. Jibelian and Dr. Jensen-Akula, both of whom told me that his condition has not improved and that he is experiencing bouts of severe depression now.

I know very well that what I am doing is for myself, and not really for him at all. I have every reason to believe that, weak as he is, he will be angry when he sees me and may make a scene that will be humiliating and frustrating for me.

And yet, it seems clear to me now, I must see him one more time before he dies. If I don't, I will have allowed myself to be put off by him from a firsthand reckoning of the reality of what is happening to him, the reality of his dying, and I think I need to see this and know this now. I have been growing increasingly dissatisfied, over these past few days, with what amounts to the emotional vacuum of remaining at a distance throughout this experience. For me it is too much like an acceptance of his own emotional block.

I realize also that what I am about to do may literally bring on or hasten his death. This also seems to me to be something I must now simply risk. In any case, Dr. Jibelian said to me on the phone yesterday that my father wanted to die now, that "the sooner the better" was what he himself felt.

Cream, our younger daughter, who is seven, particularly wanted to come with me, and after talking about it, we all agreed that she should. Her desire to go, in the first place, was greater than either Strawberry's or Armenak's. This will also be the first time I have done something special with her all by herself, whereas Strawberry made a trip to Los Angeles with me last year. As for Armenak, once I told him that he would be next in line for a special trip of some kind that just he and I would go on, he seemed satisfied to let this be Cream's trip.

She is, I think, of all of us, the one most likely by her presence alone to disarm her grandfather. On his visits with us before our estrangement, he was noticeably charmed, or, more accurately, quite visibly enchanted by her.

She is both very sweet and, underneath this sweetness, very wild—fiery. Her body is soft and light and extremely relaxed. She has periodic crying bouts during which she just seems to want to let grief pass through her, and although these can grow tiresome, they are never actually alarming—they seem to be part of her nature. She is like a second mother to Armenak and the two of them can play happily for hours together at times.

She is, in some way we are all aware of without quite being able to fathom, a profound little being. I think she knows intuitively what this situation with her grandfather is all about, and that she has some equally intuitive sense of how to handle it. I know, of course, that her magic may fail, but I trust that my father will show her his kindness. I am quite sure that she will be the youngest visitor he's had.

I spoke with Ruben yesterday, as well, and he told me that my father is sometimes asleep when visitors come and that he sometimes doesn't wake up while they are there. I'm ready for this to happen, too, and I don't think either Cream or I would be disturbed by it. Cream will be bringing him some flowers, and I will take him a book of Pasternak's last poems, the most beautiful poems I know.

Lucy called yesterday afternoon and read me a fine letter she had received from Aram Kevorkian, who was deeply upset by the pain he'd unwittingly caused her. In contrast to Wordsworth's line "The child is father of the man," he wrote, in Pop's case, "the child *is* the man"— and this was something that one simply had to accept about him. But he didn't believe, he wrote, that it was the real Bill Saroyan he knew who had done what he had done to Lucy when she had come up to be with him. Lucy began to cry as she read me the letter over the phone.

We arrived at the hospital on Wednesday afternoon at around two o'clock. I parked and Cream got out of the back seat. Her face was flushed red with the long, hot drive, five hours in all. She stood on the sidewalk for a moment, holding the bouquet of flowers Gailyn had put together for Pop. It was a garden bouquet with daisies, mint, yellow fragrant stock, and a red rose set in an old earthenware mustard jar with water in it so that it wouldn't wilt on the ride up. Cream also sprayed it periodically with our garden spray bottle during our journey.

I rolled up the windows and locked the doors on my side, and then joined her on the sidewalk. From the back seat of the car, I took out my tweed sports jacket, and put it on. Then, Cream holding the flowers while I held the book of Pasternak's poems, in which I had inserted a bookmark at the poem "After the Storm," we walked toward the hospital.

Cream was wearing a Pierre Deux dress, a present from her Grandma Carol, and black-velvet party shoes, with blue knee socks. With the jacket, I was wearing a light-blue shirt ("A healing color," Gailyn had remarked half seriously as I picked it out that morning), navy-blue corduroy pants, and my new brown-leather desert boots, which I'd polished for the first time that morning. Several steps toward the entrance, I took the bouquet from Cream because I was afraid she'd either drop it or miss a step on her way in and fall, because she was holding it —or both.

"I'll give it to you before we go in to Grandpa Bill's, honey," I told her.

"OK," she said sweetly.

On the last leg of the journey, coming down to Fresno on Route 99, I had been especially conscious that this was both "my father's country" and at the same time that it was that part of America to which so many Armenians had gravitated to begin their lives anew, finding their footholds, beginning what for some became a gradual ascent, while others only managed to get by, and still others, like my grandfather Armenak, fell by the wayside.

This was a hot, flat, sunbaked country. "GAS 'N EAT" read a crudely painted sign off the highway; then, on the other side, suddenly in a field, stood a fleet of brand-new brightly colored tractors for sale. Amidst the billboards for the Fresno motels ("Smugglers' Inn," "The Piccadilly") was one for the "Penney Newman Grain Company," the company taken over by my father's boyhood friend Frank "Yep" Moradian.

Why had he kept that name, Penney Newman, I wondered. Something American sounding, I thought, remembering Yep himself, an easygoing deep-voiced Armenian first-generation American, who had gone to elementary school with my father, as well as gone swimming naked in the San Joaquin River with him, before it had the green film over the top I had seen from the bridge as I had driven in.

I held the door for Cream and we walked out of the hot sunlight into the air-conditioned hospital, and I was immediately glad I'd put on my jacket, if only as a gesture of respect to my father for the staff, more than for he himself, to notice.

At the information desk, I asked for the nearest drinking fountain, and for the rest rooms, both of which proved to be just around the corner.

I held Cream up for a drink, and then had one myself. Cream was quiet, watching the passing inpatients and their visitors. A man went by with a severe bowl to his walk, pitching hugely from side to side as he moved forward.

"Do you want to go to the ladies' room?" I asked Cream.

She said no.

I put the bouquet of flowers on the little stone shelf out of which the drinking fountain extended and asked her to wait beside it while I went into the men's room just across from the drinking fountain.

"OK," she said quietly.

When I came out, having first splashed water on my face and checked my hair in the mirror, we went around the corner to the elevators.

There were two inpatients on board when we got on, both dressed in hospital smocks, one a middle-aged man with several days' growth of beard, and the other an older man, tall, with a friendly, humorous manner, in a wheelchair.

"The ride's free," he smiled to Cream and me.

We got off at the fourth floor, where I knew my father had his room, and I was immediately stopped by a middle-aged woman, apparently a hospital administrator because immediately after speaking to me, she walked into an office partitioned off the fourth-floor lobby.

"I'm sorry, sir, there are no children allowed in the hospital."

I followed her into the office, holding Cream's hand, where she looked up at me again.

"I'm Mr. Saroyan's son," I said. "And this is his grand-daughter, and we've just driven down from San Francisco to see him."

"I see," she said. "Well, you'll have to get permission at the nurses' station." And from the door of the office, she pointed me down the corridor.

I was stopped by several other hospital personnel on the short walk to the nurses' station, and told that there were no children allowed. I explained who I was, and each time was referred again to the nurses' station.

At the nurses' station again, a small blond man around my own age appeared and told me the same thing, and when I answered, he directed me to my father's nurse, a hefty middle-aged lady with a spirited and kindly manner who introduced herself as Lucille Kermoyan.

"Yes," she told me at once. "He knows you're coming. Let me check him."

She then went and opened the door opposite the nurses' station itself, and went into the room, closing the door behind her.

I was surprised that he knew I was coming. I had spoken to Ruben Saroyan the night before, but I hadn't said anything definite, only that I was thinking of coming up and I had asked him what he thought of the idea. He told me that my father hadn't said anything at all about me, either positive or negative, but that he was moody and had been angry that day when his cousin, and one of his closest friends, Archie Minasian, had visited, because Archie had apparently broken the story that he had had a stroke, confirming this to a *Fresno Bee* reporter who had phoned him in Palo Alto the night of the day my father had been admitted to the hospital.

I had spoken to Archie yesterday evening before I had spoken with Ruben, and he'd told me sadly that my father had been angry, but he had also said he thought

I should go up and see him, that he felt intuitively that my father would like to see me. He was alone in feeling this way. When I had called Dr. Jibelian earlier in the day, he reported that my father had told him he didn't want to see even his grandchildren.

Lucille came back out of the room now and walked over to me and Cream.

"He's still sleeping right now," she told me. "Why don't you go down to the snack bar on the third floor for a little while, say fifteen minutes. I'll be waking him up soon."

"We'd just like to see him for a minute, just to give him the flowers and the book. We don't want to tire him."

"That's fine," she said briskly, taking the bouquet out of my hands and putting it on the nurses' station counter. "We'll leave this here."

I put the book down beside it.

"How is he?" I asked her.

She looked up at me sharply now.

"He's alert," she said. "He knows exactly what's going on. He's been testing himself. Apparently he's very good at guessing the exact time, and he was upset when he was about an hour off. But I told him that for foreign surroundings, foreign diet, foreign schedule, he was very close, you know, considering."

"Yes," I said, smiling at this.

One of my father's favorite lifelong contests has been to guess the time. It is a game he plays, I imagine, by himself, and which he has also played with Lucy and me. Each of us, on a walk through Venice that summer of 1957, for instance, would guess the exact time, and he would then check his wristwatch, and whoever was closest would be the winner. There was no prize—none, that is, but my father's high regard for the relevance of this procedure, as well as for any reasonably good guess. He usually won.

He played this same game with me on my thirtieth birthday, September 25, 1973, when I took a walk with him in San Francisco on a windy, intermittently sunny day, a walk I remember now because he kept stopping to use public facilities to urinate. He did this perhaps three or four times over the course of a walk that lasted perhaps just over an hour, departing from Cosette's house at the top of the Sunset District and eventually returning there.

He never offered any explanation for his stopping this way, and I didn't ask him for any. I didn't want to embarrass him, of course. But now, I wonder, too, if I didn't believe, in my heart of hearts, that whatever physical inconveniences my father might endure as he grew older, he was still, essentially, indestructible.

When we played the game on that windy fall day, and I made a particularly good guess, he paid me his highest tribute in these matters.

"You're in the groove," he told me.

When the elevator door opened, as Cream and I stood waiting to take it down to the third floor, and a group of people emerged, I saw in their midst a small dark man with a slightly Oriental cast to his eyes smiling warmly at me and realized immediately that it was Ruben Saroyan, whom I don't remember meeting before, but who, along with Harry Bagdasarian has been looking after my father, visiting him daily, screening visitors, reading him his mail, and generally taking care of things for him since he has been in the hospital.

We introduced ourselves, shaking hands (his own hand cupped and strong in its grip), and he greeted Cream. After telling him what Lucille had told me, I asked him if he would like to join us at the snack bar, but he said he wanted to check on my father first, and perhaps would see us down there in a few minutes.

In the snack bar, Cream got Hawaiian Punch and I got a piece of pumpkin pie. We sat down in the brightly lit white Formica eating area, in a no-smoking alcove where only one other person was seated (smoking), and we were finished with our food almost immediately. I took our tray and dishes to a service wagon, and then returned to our table and took Cream's hand and we walked through the eating area, lingering for a moment at the food and drink machines, as if, perhaps, we might want to buy something more. But neither of us were actually hungry, and we went back up in the elevator now, still early for Lucille. We ended up sitting in the fourth-floor lobby for five minutes.

Two older men in wheelchairs greeted each other, one surrounded in the lobby by his family, the other on his way to the elevator.

"Have you heard about Bill Stevenson?" the one with his family called to the other, as he was manuevering his wheelchair, directly in front of the bench where Cream and I sat, to get on the elevator.

"No," the other answered. Some people had gotten on the elevator, and he called to them, "Would you hold that for me?"

"He's in 416."

"No kidding," the man in front of us answered. "Well, I'll go pay him a call."

"Well, don't wait too long. He's getting transferred to Berkeley on Monday."

By now, the man was advancing into the elevator.

"Thanks for telling me," he said. "I'll go see him right away."

*   *   *

The elevator doors closed, and I got up and took Cream's hand, and we walked back to the nurses' station, where I found Ruben Saroyan leaning against the wall just opposite my father's door.

Lucille came up and told me she would check my father now, and she went into his room.

Ruben and I traded a little family history, as I held Cream's hand. We were third cousins. He was from my father's mother Takoohi's side of the family. He had owned a grocery store for twenty-five years, and then retired on his Social Security. Like Harry, he was a bachelor. The two had also seen after my father's father Armenak's brother, Mihran, when he had had to go into the hospital, where he had then lived for six months before dying, in the late sixties.

Lucille came out now.

"OK," she said to me and Cream. "You can go in now."

I handed Cream the bouquet of flowers in the mustard jar off the nurses' station counter, and she walked to and then into his door. I wanted my father to see her first.

On the drive up, I had tried to imagine what I would do if my father responded unfavorably when we walked into the room: "Oh, no—no, no, Aram . . . No, no, no . . ."

I sensed that I was now taking things into my own hands, and that if I was going to come up and see him against his own explicit wishes, I had better be ready with *something* if the visit began on the wrong foot.

I knew that Cream would probably guarantee at least a brief visit, but I couldn't be absolutely positive even of this. I hadn't seen my father in more than three and a half years, and now he was dying. He had kicked his own daughter out of the house, and there was no telling for certain what his reaction might be to me. I knew, for instance, that he might feel deeply humiliated to see me in the condition he was in now.

I had decided to walk in behind Cream, letting him see her and the bouquet of flowers first. I would follow then, holding the book of poems. If he said anything negative, I planned to bring my finger to my mouth and "shush" him quickly, while at the same time, with my other hand, pointing to Cream.

"Behave yourself, Grandpa," I was going to say in a gently chiding voice. "This is your granddaughter."

I had now picked the book of Pasternak's poems off the counter of the nurses' station and was following Cream, who had already vanished into the room, somewhat tentatively. The more Pop sees of her before he sees me, I thought, the better chance I have.

"You come too, now!" Lucille said from outside the door, seeing me lagging behind.

I walked into the room.

Cream was approaching my father's bed at the far end of his private room, next to the windows, holding the bouquet out in front of her like a little Sunday-school acolyte.

Nothing anybody had told me had prepared me for the difference in my father's body, and equally, or even more so, in his face. From all the reports I had gotten through Lucy, his doctors, and other relatives, I had imagined that he looked somehow more or less as he always had, if perhaps understandably a bit thinner.

But his entire physiognomy had undergone a complete transformation by the time I saw him. His body was like a tattered remnant of itself. His once large arms were shriveled to the bone. He leaned up now in his bed, bracing himself against one elbow, keeping his focus restricted to Cream.

"This is your granddaughter, Cream," Lucille said.

The change in my father's face, which I saw now as he looked out at Cream, was so fundamental that it was as if his illness represented a completely new phase of his life.

He was gaunt. All the extra fluids and tissue in his face, and there had been little to begin with, had gone now. And his eyes were larger and more beautiful than I had ever before seen them, even in the photographs of him as a small child, and even in the photographs of his first fame—when he had, in fact, as my mother remarked, looked something like the young Al Pacino.

His whole aspect, perhaps heightened by his old-fashioned and now entirely white moustache, reminded me instantly of a Mathew Brady photograph of a wounded Civil War veteran. As he looked from Cream to Lucille, I could see clearly that, like the man in the Brady photograph, he had had, or was still in fact in the midst of, a close brush with death. He looked out now with the immensity of that experience, its fundamental mystery, inside him.

"Say hello to your Grandpa, Cream," Lucille said. "Oh, and isn't this a lovely bouquet she brought you?"

Lucille took the bouquet from Cream and put it on the bed table. There were a number of other, larger bouquets from florists in the room.

"Hi, Grandpa," Cream said sweetly and shyly with a little smile.

"Why don't you give your Grandpa a kiss now?" Lucille said. "Go ahead. You can just climb right up—well, here . . ."

And she began to lift Cream under the shoulders to move her toward my father—but she was stopped almost immediately by my father's arm, slowly lifted out at her.

His voice followed now, entirely changed in its rhythmic character, slower now, and almost stuttered in its pauses, but with its particular deep resonance still there, if not in fact even more striking now, in its slightly delayed arrival.

"Don't you hurt my granddaughter," he told Lucille loudly.

The poor woman immediately put Cream down.

"Oh, I would never hurt her. You know that."

"Don't you ever hurt her . . ." my father repeated now, with the last of this momentum.

After the shock of his physical change, these first words of his brought me toward some sense of his spiritual condition, which was both reassuringly familiar and even, under the circumstances, rather endearing.

He had simply taken a shot for the gallery on that one, done a quick, apparently irresistible turn as a road company Kit Carson in *The Time of Your Life,* now on his deathbed.

He was dramatic, that's all. He had made a life out of it, and even now, in his final days, if he saw an opening, he took a shot at it.

"And . . ." Lucille turned toward me now, bringing up the rear into the room. "You know your son . . ."

Now, for the first time, my father turned to me, and our eyes met. According to Cream, he now remarked what I have in fact no memory of hearing, since I was perhaps at this moment too caught up in *seeing* him to pay much attention to the words that were spoken: "I'll never forget him . . ."

That first look he gave me was both more naked than any I had ever seen from him before, and at the same time more defiant.

Here he was, I thought, in this sunbaked vineyard country, the homegrown artist, the special treasure of this now prosperous American town, barely more than an immigrant settlement when he was born here, now old, now dying, fussed over and prized to his last for, among other things, those two very elements I saw in his eyes now—their nakedness and, in the face of what he might take to be some untoward ambiguity in my presence, their defiance.

"Hi, Pop," I said, finding my voice already almost choked with emotion, the emotion I had been having so much trouble keeping track of during all the days before I had seen him.

I approached his vicinity lightly, keeping a kind of tentative, reversible dimension in my movements. I didn't want to scare him. I didn't want to lock horns.

"I brought you a book," I said, laying Pasternak's poems down beside Cream's bouquet on the table.

He didn't give the book even a glance. I hadn't expected him to. If, in fact, he was still reading, which there was little evidence of—there was a stack of copies of *Obituaries,* and one of *Chance Meetings,* and one of *Letters from 74 Rue Taitbout,* about five copies in each stack, on a shelf on the wall opposite his bed, and there was a stack of letters beside these, but no other books or reading material—if he was still reading, I hoped he would pick up the book sometime in privacy, and read the poem where I had placed the bookmark.

There was also a cover photograph of Pasternak, shortly before he died, standing in the sunlight, holding a package in his hand and looking out at the world in the middle of an ambiguous gesture. To me, the package looked like a loaf of bread and I couldn't tell whether Pasternak had just accepted it, or was passing it on to each viewer of the photograph.

The title of the book seemed to have a resonance in itself. *In the Interlude,* it was called, poems 1945–1960, the final poems of Pasternak's life.

Lucille excused herself after another moment or two, leaving the three of us together.

"You have a nice visit now," she said to us all, closing the door as she left.

"We don't want to tire you out, Pop," I said as I moved to the sink by the door, and cupped my hands to drink some water from the faucet. "So just tell me when you want me to go."

I wanted him to know, up front, that this was not a state of siege—physically, or emotionally. He didn't reply to this directly, but when I returned to his bed, he asked me to give him some of his cranberry juice.

"It's over here," he said, pointing to the cup on the table. "You hold it for me."

Standing next to his bed table, I leaned forward to bring the cup close to his face so that he could suck through the straw. I was happy to see that my hands weren't shaking.

Suddenly Lucille was back in the room for something, and I withdrew the cup as he opened his mouth to speak to her.

"Can I get some more juice?" he asked her. There was only a little left in the cup.

"Sure," she said, looking at him. "What would you like?"

"More cranberry," he said.

"All right." She fussed for a moment with a Shasta and a lemon soda in cans already on his bed table.

"You know," she told him, "for that indigestion you've got, sometimes these are good for settling the stomach."

Then she began to leave, but hesitated near the door, waiting for his response.

"It's not that they're good or bad," my father said to her. "It's that they're irrelevant."

"All right," she said cheerily, about to go out the door. "Or would you like some orange juice?"

"No, cranberry," he said firmly.

Ruben had told me in our conversation outside the door that my father, because of the cancer in his liver, no longer had taste buds. Before coming up, I had heard from his doctors that he was eating very few solids of any kind anymore, and that this seemed to affect his condition negatively, but that he apparently couldn't be persuaded to go on eating. In commenting that the different juices, and their effects, were irrelevant, I took him to be saying to Lucille—and perhaps, it occurred to me, he meant this more for me than for her—simply that he was dying.

Alone in the room with us again, my father told Cream how much he loved her mother's paintings, which he had presumably seen most recently in the photographs in our scrapbook, in which there were several pages devoted to Gailyn's show this fall in Beverly Hills.

"She's a wonderful painter," I said, nodding to Pop, once again barely able to control my voice. God, I thought, I hope I don't end up wailing at his bedside.

"Yes, she is," he answered, nodding back at me. "They are absolutely radiant. Even in that . . ." Here he hesitated, and his hand went up in the effort to articulate. ". . . darkness . . ."

And now his thought broke, and he seemed to have difficulty breathing. Could he have been referring to the darkness of his tract house on Easter Sunday when he had gotten our scrapbook, perhaps the very day he had lapsed into unconsciousness, although not discovered until the next morning, the scrapbook lying on the table where his head had fallen? There was a blue and reddish blood line now in the middle of his forehead, perhaps a mark of the moment his head had fallen.

Now he turned his attention back to Cream, who had remained standing beside his bed, near the end of it, because his bed table made it impossible for her to stand any closer on that side.

"What does *your* father do?" he asked her.

This was a deliberate jibe at me, a questioning of my own identity that was part and parcel of our perennial relationship.

"What?" Cream answered, most likely confused by the question.

"What does *your* father do?" Pop enunciated clearly to her once again.

She paused a moment, thinking it over.

"He writes screenplays," she said then, but too softly for him to hear.

He looked up at me.

"What did she say?"

"She said, 'He writes screenplays,' " I answered, with a slight smile.

"Ah," he nodded, without making any more of it.

"How are you, Cream?" I smiled at her, squeezing her shoulders to make sure she knew everything was all right. She gave me a good smile back. She was fine.

I myself was at loose ends and, worried that I was too unsettled for the moment, and that my father would become upset by my presence, I suddenly noticed the upholstered chair against the wall parallel to the head of his bed, and, with the sense of taking a deliberate measure, I sat down in it, more or less out of his sight.

There was a chair against the opposite wall as well, near the shelf with my father's books, and after a moment or two, I asked Cream if she wouldn't like to sit down in it.

This wouldn't, as in my own case, remove her from my father's sight. He would still be able to see her clearly from his bed, and it might relax him not to see her standing any longer in front of him.

Cream sat down now, too.

For some time there was quiet, or, more accurately, the only noise was my father's breathing, which would sometimes grow quite loud, as if he were straining for air. Then, sporadically, he would make a sudden noise almost like a shout, as if to clear the passage of his breath. He also seemed to be swallowing over and over again, as if he had a burp that wouldn't quite materialize.

Suddenly a young man appeared at the door, looking in.

"Oh," he said. "I won't bother you now while you're visiting."

"No," my father said, waving him into the room.

He walked around to the other side of my father's bed and stood looking at my father.

"This is my son," my father said.

I stood up and came forward, and Cream stood up beside me.

"Hello," said the young man, who was dark with thick-cropped hair. "I'm Dr. Aduan."

"Hello," I said, not shaking his hand because it would involve reaching across the bed.

"And this is his daughter," Pop said, looking at Cream, "my granddaughter."

Then, after a pause, he added, "Her name is Cream."

"Cream?" the young doctor asked.

"Yes," my father answered.

"Well," he said. "That's a nice name."

"Thank you," Cream said.

I now began to move back toward my chair, to give the doctor room for whatever his business might be, and Cream did likewise.

"Strawberry" and "Cream," two vintage names from the era of flower children, names about which my father had been at best ambivalent, had been, paradoxically, neither my own nor Gailyn's idea, but my mother's, sent to us in a list of possibilities during Gailyn's first two pregnancies, which we had gradually over the course of considering alternatives of our own come to find irresistible. My mother, in fact, does have something of the sensibility of an evolved flower child. I wondered if my father had ever suspected that the names had come from her.

"Well," the doctor said, looking at my father, "you seem to be more yourself today."

My father now seemed to be happy to have the doctor to talk to in the midst of our visit, almost as if he could talk *through* him to me and Cream, whereas I was feeling more and more certain that our own visit wouldn't involve much talking. He had some apparent difficulty speaking, but his words all came out very clearly enunciated, if often in a halting, staggered progression.

"I make . . . no demands," he said. "I'm . . . letting go. Well, somebody said, maybe that's not the right thing to do. And I said—maybe it isn't. I don't know. I'm grappling with the mystery of . . . what . . . *is.*"

Like the comment about the drinks being irrelevant, to Lucille, this was apparently both more and less than the doctor seemed to know what to do with, and he took a new tack.

"Your brother phoned—again," he said.

"There's a sorrow in that," my father said. My God, I thought, it's as if he's writing even now. "Because . . ." And here he made a gesture into the room toward Cream, now sitting in her chair again. ". . . this," he said, looking at Cream, "this is *beautiful.*"

I wasn't aware of the meaning of this exchange until after our visit had ended, and I had returned home. Gailyn told me then that she had gotten a phone call at around noon, long after we'd left, from my Aunt Cosette, saying that she had heard from my Uncle Henry, and that I wasn't to go up to see my father. She told Gailyn that she had understood that I was going up to interview my father for a magazine article.

Who could have come up with this? No one other than Gailyn and my sister know that I am keeping this journal, and, in any case, there was no possibility whatsoever of "interviewing" Pop about anything. The air was so charged with our past conflicts that silence was an order we each accepted by default. The emotional chaos between us was just too enormous, and he was now too weak in any case, to waste time trying to put it in order.

It was now a case of make do, or die—and we both knew the dying was going to happen whether we were able to make do, or not.

His little stab at me by way of the question to Cream —that bold, self-amused razzing of me, my life, my work —was, in fact, a throwaway with no more energy behind it than the "Don't you ever hurt my granddaughter" grandstanding to Lucille.

He was, in this sense, a shadow of his former self. But in the absence of the true substance of that self, the air was charged with the potential of our silence.

*   *   *

And Cream is quite masterful with silence. It is her element in some special way—she isn't bored by it and made impatient, as many children can be.

When the doctor left, saying he'd drop in again tomorrow for another visit, the three of us began to get down to business in earnest.

There was no more talking. Pop had said his piece, about letting go. Sitting in the chair and following his breathing, and my own, and even playing at synchronizing them, I did consider a few good-natured platitudes like "I really think you're doing this right, Pop." But I knew in my heart that just wasn't the way the wind was blowing.

I looked over at Cream on her chair, more or less to check in with a little eye contact, but she was by now quite beyond the pale.

She was looking into the middle distance a bit above me as if she were asleep and awake at the same time, or perhaps alive and dead at the same time, but let me make no preposterous claims for a child's simplicity and grace, except to say that it became obvious after a while that the three of us were involved in a kind of group meditation.

Then, abruptly, Lucille burst back into the room and was understandably a little put off by the absence of any verbal atmosphere. She immediately addressed Cream.

"You know you can *talk* to your Grandpa." And she moved around to the side of his bed where the doctor had stood, and held some more cranberry juice for him to drink. "Why don't you come around here?"

Cream, essentially undisturbed, obeyed her, going to stand by him on the other side of his bed where she could be closer to him.

At this point, I said something to the effect that perhaps she could tell her Grandpa Bill something about her school, a suggestion that sank like a stone within the already deeper fluencies in the room.

We were all, including apparently Pop, listening to my father—as if, in effect, listening to the special, invisible guest in our midst, which was Death itself.

Lucille left again, and now it really began to get strong. For a moment, I considered the title *Obituaries* and how it was a kind of self-fulfilling prophecy to have that as the final title of one's published writing, and, at the same time, to me, a warning to watch the titles one uses as "readings" on one's state of being generally. How could he revive from a title like that? Or had he purposefully, in effect, buried himself alive?

Henry had informed me that Pop had, in fact, made arrangements with the Neptune Society to have his body cremated. There was to be no funeral; and the ashes were to be scattered however they do. ("No fuss / No bother / No mess / No father"—four lines that came to me when I heard this, a week or so before.)

I made a final effort on behalf of Cream.

"Would you like a Shasta or a lemon soda, honey?" I asked her, leaning forward to catch her eye across the bed.

She declined wordlessly.

My father in his bed continued staring roughly forward as she stood by his side.

I leaned back in my chair again and gradually let go.

I was breathing with him now, and I'd given up any further thought of conversational gambits.

He had the hiccoughs for a while, and, a little while later, he cut a long, rather peaceful fart. I remembered that this had never been much in the way of a comic event even in the old days, when Lucy and I had shared space with him on summer vacations.

I tried to remember to keep my breathing regular and deep, as his was, and just let things pass, without distracting him or myself or Cream any further with even a turn of the head. Keep a steady beat, simply, and let it be.

Suddenly I was just another person breathing in the room, and one of the other two people also breathing in it was my father, seventy-two, and the other person was my daughter, seven and a half.

We were now, all of us, steady as she goes.

In a little while, I heard Cream make a little step here, a little step there, the lightest pitter-patter of her being decorating the air, as if she had put one foot up and then down and then the other, and then turned around to look out the window, and I suddenly felt as if my father and I, lying and sitting parallel with each other, were parts of a single molecular structure, and Cream, like some newly emerged electric particle of our whole unit, danced between us—the *new generation* of our matter itself, as Pop lay dying, and I sat, at thirty-seven, in the middle of the process he was ending and she was beginning.

And then it came to me all at once that we were being the chain I had envisioned several days before, the one my father had never quite been able to link up with, as it had seemed to me then, since the loss of his father had linked him into oblivion on *both sides,* not allowing him to be the beginning link in a series of three generations —child/father/father's father; emigration and the American experience eliminating both the second and the third. But I would swear to it that right now, in the last moments of his life, we were linking up, with me in the middle.

And, in a curious way, perhaps the same curious way

that his face now was younger and more naked than I had ever before seen it, it was almost as if he were both dying now and being born, too.

In fact, hadn't he told *The New York Times Book Review,* in a feature they'd run on writers' new works, that he wanted to do a book now, after *Obituaries,* called *Births,* the other side of the chain linking into oblivion?

We were, in this moment, all at once, it seemed to me, the family we had never been.

I wondered if he felt it. I wondered if it was time to go. I wondered if he'd in fact by now fallen asleep, but I couldn't afford to move my head to look at him. It might make him self-conscious and break the spell.

And then, suddenly, my father reached up to the bar suspended over his bed and held it to turn over on his side toward Cream.

In the car, on our way home, Cream told me that he took her hand at this point.

"He was afraid I was going to hold his hand too hard and hurt him, so I made my hand very soft."

This is remarkable to me, because I have never known Cream's hands *not* to be soft, with long, thin, sculptured fingers, in their shape more like my father's own hands, in fact, than anyone else's in our family; though my father's hands, in addition to their beauty, had a strong, workmanlike, substantial quality.

She told me he was playing with her hand in his hand —playing with her hand instead of *speaking* to her, I guessed out loud on the ride back, telling her little stories directly to her nervous system itself, so newly emerged from what he would soon again merge with, after his whole big life.

An old storyteller and his little granddaughter in the Fresno four P.M.

*   *   *

And then he was breathing more deeply, and I started wondering again if he'd fallen to sleep, closed his eyes (I had heard that my cousin Hank, Henry's son, had come up and sat with him for an hour and he'd never opened his eyes). And, all at once, I sensed that our visit was over, and I got up out of my chair, and looked over at Cream, and asked her softly, trying to pantomime it as well—closing my eyes, making my hands a pillow, and resting my head on it—if her Grandpa was asleep; but she didn't understand, so I had to say it louder.

"Is he asleep?"

Cream nodded, and I walked around to the other side of his bed, and saw his eyes closed, his face nestled between the white side bars of his hospital bed.

"Why don't you kiss your Grandpa good-bye?" I suggested to Cream.

She told me on the ride home, as the sun fell across the green gently rolling slopes just above San Joaquin County, that when he told Lucille to put her down, she thought he didn't want her to kiss him—so she hesitated now.

"Where?" she said.

"His forehead," I said quietly.

But this would have been perhaps too awkward for her in her ambivalence, having to manuever down a bit, and she ended up kissing him quickly on his hair, and I saw his eyes open with a small start as she did.

Would I now kiss him?

I decided I would kiss the top of his forehead, where I had pointed Cream, and moved forward toward him. He looked up at me as if momentarily confused by my coming forward.

I moved toward his forehead and said "Good-bye, Pop," just before kissing him.

*　　*　　*

And then, without hesitation, he flung his arm over my shoulder as I leaned over him, and the kiss turned into a hug. Suddenly I found myself holding my dying father. How light he was! And instead of feeling the density of muscle at the back of his neck, as I had known it all my life, it was *soft* there, the flesh relaxed to my hand. In that moment, he seemed to surrender and almost to melt into me as I held him. I wanted consciously to let him feel both my firmness and strength, and yet, at the same time, I wanted him to know that I was gentle and easy.

"Thank you, Aram," he said, his voice deep with emotion, the long-withheld words suddenly real now on the air.

"Thank *you,* Pop," I answered, feeling my own emotion swell. I felt instantaneously that we were speaking both in the moment and at the same time saying goodbye for our whole lives.

"It's the most beautiful time of my life . . . and death."

"For me, too, Pop," I answered, now literally crying.

And then—it had been perhaps twenty seconds in all that I had held him—I released him gently onto the bed. And Cream and I left the room.

As I was closing his door, now outside in the corridor, I heard him saying loudly, "It's unbelievable! . . . It's unbelievable!" For a moment, I considered going back in again, but, in the end, I continued with Cream down the hospital corridor.

The next day, Thursday, after getting home with Cream asleep in the back of the Volvo station wagon at around ten on Wednesday night, I woke up still amazed by the visit, and lay in bed as the sun came out in the garden, which I watched through the windows in our back bedroom.

It was the final thing he had not yet done with me, the missing thing all his life—except in the moment of his art —that surrender that had so frightened him. Now, as he let himself go to Death, as he broke all the holds on his being and let himself flow into the final mystery of his "life . . . and death," it was possible to him.

"It's unbelievable," he had all but shouted. It was almost as if he were speaking of having found some new possibility that deeply challenged his previous assumptions. I wonder, in fact, if the sort of wholehearted communion we had shared isn't, after all, the only real immortality around, if it isn't in surrender, rather than in holding on or, as he would have it, "not dying," that we truly meet the eternal.

He was to me, in this sense, quite literally in this final phase of his life a more evolved and generous man than he had been able to be before now. The fact that he could surrender to me as he did was something very like a miracle to me. It was as if he were saying, at long last, you are a man, I love you, let me give you the legacy of

my emotion, let me melt and merge into you, my son and
my heir.

I was crying again as I dressed. How brave he had
been, in his way. He had stayed alive long enough to
know that I no longer needed him, and in fact would no
longer accept his censure—the only form his love could
ever seem to take—and then, finally, when he knew that
for certain, when I would no longer reply, or argue, or
protest in any form, when I was completely detached
from all the forms by which he made himself known to
me, when I had, to all intents and purposes, discarded
him, let him go, let him go to die when he would die—
well, then, in fact, as I intuitively sensed he might, then
he did, in earnest, begin to die.

But perhaps I had sensed wrongly the quality of this
dying, at least as the evidence of his actual approach to
death, as well as my own visit with him, might suggest.
For now in a certain sense he knew he had done his job,
not only as an artist, but as a father as well. I had told him,
in any case, that I wanted no more of him; I had released
him now from any further parental obligation.

And perhaps it *was,* quite literally, a release. He had
lived for seven decades, and at least half of that life was
full of awful anguish, killing despair.

Now, at last, he could let go and begin to die.

The summer I was seventeen years old, I had joined
him in Paris, and we were going to spend the summer
together while Lucy went to camp in Montana.

By now, I knew myself to be quite deeply sick, but I'd
begun, tentatively but seriously, the gradual turning in
upon myself that was also, in my case, a turning *into*
myself, a becoming.

I had an uneasy sense of being blocked—the summer

before, in my first attempt to "go all the way," I had found myself impotent, a common enough occurrence but one I took to heart with uncommon finality—and yet, at the same time, forced in upon myself as I was, I sensed a new spectrum of possibilities.

Perhaps, after all, the reason I couldn't sleep with a girl was that I didn't know who I was, and perhaps I didn't know, in turn, because I was, in fact, *nobody*. I felt a dark, in fact a black chaos in myself, and now, after this first failure—a huge self-affirmed DEATH right at the beginning of my life—now, perhaps, I could both learn who I really was and (the other side of the coin) educate myself *into* being at the same time.

That summer we decided to drive down the southern coast of France, into Spain and then into Italy, but three or four days gone in his red Kharmann Ghia, he had opened up on my mother again, and now, fearing quite literally that I would be turned off women *for good* by his second sustained assault (my idea was once I got to know myself, maybe *then* I could get to know a woman, and it would work), I became constipated, and nothing seemed to bring this condition to an end.

I was holding myself rigid, fearing he would change me in a way I didn't want to be changed.

My mother had had an almost impossible time trying to reestablish her identity to me after the 1957 summer, finally enlisting the support of a family friend, the late Arnold Krakower, a lawyer who had been so earnestly and almost poetically appalled at my father's distortions that, in a voice as loud and as clear as my father's own, and with reserves of genuine goodness I couldn't help but be aware of in his manner, he had somehow managed to dispel most of the darkness in several talks with me in his midtown Manhattan law office. He was a man I could admire, who gave me his help, his attention. Another angel in my own life.

I remember walking through some nameless town on the coast of Spain, in the darkness after a big hotel dinner, crying as my father went on helplessly. I remember one night in a hotel room, still talking, still arguing, even after we'd turned off the lights, and there was only the play of light from the street below decorating areas of the room off and on. My father now, after a few moments of quiet, suddenly began to sob in deep, choked spasms, so that at first I wasn't sure exactly what was happening. It was the first and last time I have ever known him to cry.

And then, about two weeks into the trip, which had turned into compulsive, nonstop driving and his venting of anger at my mother, I decided I wanted to go back to New York. I said it before we went to sleep one night, and, almost surprised by my own conviction, I repeated it the next morning.

He drove me in silence to a town in Spain. I got a bus to Madrid, where I took a plane back to New York. He wouldn't speak to me on the sunny drive along the highway, nor would he let me drive, a practice of our previous days. I remained silent.

Then, as I was about to board the bus, he hugged me and kissed me and put a twenty-dollar gold piece in my hand.

"Keep it," he said quietly, with a weight of all that was unspoken between us. "It's good luck."

I took it and got on the bus to Madrid and got the plane and, in a matter of hours, was back again inside my own screwed-up life. I have always thought of this as the first decision of my adult life.

The gold piece, as I remember, like others that he had collected, was dated 1874: the year of Armenak's birth.

But this man *lived* all these years, hours, perhaps even minutes to him, day by day, jotting down the minutiae of their passing in his page-a-day diary; he *lived* when his whole world had died for him long since, until his son could, at long last, and possibly even to his final eternal relief, *reject* him, tell him to fuck off you stupid son of a bitch, I don't want you, I don't need you, I never want to see you again.

Then he let go.

He held on all that time to make sure he was not another Armenak. And he succeeded, he performed to the very best of his ability, I am quite certain now, and if his emotional assets took the frozen form of twenty-dollar gold pieces and whatever other means he could claim, they were nevertheless the real thing: they were his very own gold.

He acted. And if he could not *re*act, it gave him more pain than I will ever be able to honestly assess. Pain that he lived with day by day.

I knew on Thursday morning that I had to phone Lucy, and tell her what had happened, though I had considered the night before not doing it, letting it go until I heard from her. I knew that she would probably be upset, jealous, etc.—these feelings would be helpless on her part, and understandable—but I also knew that there was at least a fifty-fifty chance that she could see him now and have a decent visit, and I knew that this would be important to Pop, if he were able to carry it through, as well as to Lucy.

Archie Minasian, my father's cousin and lifelong pal, was delighted by the news that my visit had gone well, and told me on the phone: "I couldn't be more thrilled if a man from outer space landed and came up to me and told me a secret."

Archie, the loud and laughing poet, could break my father up as no one else ever could. His alter ego, "Archie Crashcup," the persona of numberless comic routines, was a man who stood behind the cosmic eight ball with endless, if bewildered goodwill. Archie, in the end, was the only relative in what Gailyn remarked the other night was a family as full of intrigue and secretiveness as a Medici court, to wish my father reconciliation with his children.

He told me on the phone he was sure Pop wanted to see Lucy. The father of six children himself, he said that he couldn't imagine any worse pain than what a parent feels in rejecting a child.

Thursday, for the most part, was spent on the phone. Lucy finally spoke with Gailyn and asked her to let me go with her, which Gailyn and I agreed to—and, for a while, it looked as if I would go. Then, as evening came on, and Lucy grew more afraid, remembering her last visit, it looked as if she wouldn't go at all.

But yesterday morning she phoned to say that she was on her way with her friend Berry Berenson. And last night, at around six, the good news came through that it had gone well.

He had told everyone that he didn't want to see her; but then, on hearing she was actually there, he'd asked impatiently, "Where is she?"

She was allowed in.

Seeing her, Pop said, "I'm a dying man. I can't take this . . ."

Lucy told him she didn't want to talk, she just wanted them to spend a little time together.

She applied cold compresses to his forehead, and he made noises of pleasure. He held her hand between his own hands with his eyes closed. He melted, and received, and gave, with Lucy, too.

"Who is Cream?" he asked her.

"She's Aram's second daughter," she told him.

"Out of this world," he answered. "Out of this world."

"Do you love me, Pop?" Lucy asked him quietly.

He nodded.

Tomorrow, we will drive up as a family so that we can visit him with Strawberry and Armenak, too.

Lucy may come up again later on.

"Good to see you," my father said immediately, looking over at me from his bed, as I entered his hospital room, holding Armenak's hand, yesterday afternoon at around three.

"Good to see you too, Pop," I answered.

He was unshaven this time, grizzled, and his eyes seemed smaller, but he was in fine spirits.

I led Armenak around to the far side of my father's bed. The little blond blue-eyed four-year-old boy hasn't seen his Grandpa since he was scarcely a year old.

My father reached out as if he was going to kiss him, but then just held his hand to Armenak's forehead. I decided not to lift him to kiss his Grandpa just yet. My son's expression was serious, somewhat baffled, and I knew he was a bit uneasy.

"This is a great man," my father said. "He's *hot.*"

I noticed the nasal western twang in my father's voice this time; I had heard it the first time, but it hadn't struck me as fully.

Gailyn and the girls now appeared at the door.

"Hello, Gailyn. Hello, Strawberry. Hello, Cream," Pop said.

Gailyn came around to the side of his bed and Pop reached up and kissed her warmly on the mouth. Strawberry and Cream remained, a bit tentatively, in the middle of the room. Then after a moment everyone seemed to settle in this middle area of the room as Pop spoke, looking at me as I stood near the end of his bed.

"They're trying to shave my *soul,*" he told us, refer-ring to his whiskers. "But I tell them that's all that's left, and I like to leave it."

"You look beautiful, Pop," I told him sincerely.

"Well," he said, "I don't deserve this beautiful family. I don't know about these kids sitting here, witnessing this scene of Dickensian preposterousness."

"We're so happy to see you," Gailyn said.

My father then, in fact, proceeded to do a turn as the Dickensian grandfather on his deathbed, and yet one of such untamed animal spirits that he ended up reminding me again of Kit Carson in *The Time of Your Life.*

"Let me see the kids now," he said, and the three of them readied themselves for his scrutiny.

"Strawberry," he all but shouted, "you're beautiful. You're the greatest of us all. Cream, you're the deepest mystery, untellable. Armenak, you're a ball of energy, ready to explode!"

His hand made a flourish with this final pronouncement.

"I don't deserve this!" he roared. "It's too much to ask for, more than I could ask for. The worst damn fool in the world—and a good boy."

I burst out laughing at this paradoxical self-characteri-zation, but Gailyn told us all later that she thought the "good boy" part referred to me.

"Now, who is Cream?" he asked the room at large.

Gailyn told me later that she was tempted here to answer that she felt that Cream combined the best quali-ties of both my father and my mother, but sensing, most likely accurately, that this would disturb him, she an-swered instead, "She's an angel."

My father nodded, taking this in.

*   *   *

After a few more moments, sensing that Pop would tire, Gailyn and Strawberry and Armenak left the room, while I remained behind with Cream to speak to him for a moment more quietly and more seriously.

"Your father wants to speak to *his* father," he explained to Armenak as the little boy was leaving.

I suppose I asked Cream to stay because I wanted to reestablish something of the sincerity of our first meeting. Also, I suppose, I was still a little uncertain of his responses and I knew Cream's presence would soften any disharmony that might arise.

"Lucy phoned, Pop. I'm glad you had a good visit."

"Now," he said loudly. "Let me ask you to speak up because I'm still half deaf."

I had started to tell him the same thing about Lucy's visit while everybody was in the room and had been mysteriously but decisively interrupted by him, offering the information that he had lifesavers in his mouth as a general medicine.

I'd interpreted this to mean that I had opened the conversation in a direction he didn't want it to go, at least with all of us in the room. Now I understood that he hadn't heard me, and in an effort not to let things slide, had covered for himself with this spontaneous revelation.

Speaking louder now, I told him I was glad to hear about Lucy's visit.

"I have nothing but the highest respect for the bravery of that girl, after what happened, coming up a second time."

This was unexpectedly straightforward, and encouraged, I now told him what I had wanted to say, but hadn't been certain it was quite the right time.

"The way you're doing this, Pop, is very natural—and

very powerful. And we'd all like to go through it with you together."

I kept my voice loud. He listened.

"Now, I just want to mention this, in case it's a possibility, and if it isn't, there's no problem. Would it be possible for us to use your corner house to stay in when we come down, and then we could visit you more often and more regularly?"

Archie had told me on the phone that it was this house my father used to put up visitors when they stayed overnight.

"Don't worry about your papers or anything," I added immediately. "Nobody will take or disturb anything. It's just a place with a kitchen and a backyard for the kids . . ."

I had discussed this idea with Archie on the phone, to get his sense of it, and he'd been immediately and enthusiastically for it.

"I'd love it," my father said now. "We could all be together."

"Right," I said. "And Lucy wants to come up."

"Lucy has *got* to be here," he said with clear emphasis.

So, in the first blush of his response, he had been for it. But I knew my father to sometimes say something positive only to cut short an uncomfortable encounter. Now, in fact, he began to explore negative dimensions.

"I can't ask it," he said solemnly.

"I know you can't ask it, Pop," I said boldly, my hand out on the air. "But if you'll *accept* it . . ."

"Lucy is a very busy woman," he said.

"She's not busy," I said. "Not too busy for this. She loves you very much, Pop. She could stay in the house. And we could come down as a family. Or sometimes I could just come down."

"All right, now," he said, calling the discussion to a close. "Let's have everybody in again."

I went to get Gailyn, Strawberry, and Armenak, while Cream waited in the room. We all said good-bye warmly. As Gailyn and the children were leaving the room, I went around to the far end of his bed and kissed my father and he kissed me.

"So, can I call Ruben and Lucy?" I asked him. I didn't know whether he would refuse the whole idea now.

"Sure," he said, casually. "Whatever you want to do."

I patted his knee under the sheet and began to leave the room.

"OK, Pop," I said. "See you soon."

Outside in the corridor, he had another visitor waiting. A man with a large moustache, who looked something like my father, and his wife, a pretty dark-haired woman in her fifties. His name was Karny Saroyan.

"Are you Aram?" the man asked me.

"Yes," I said.

"You look just like your father," he told me.

"I was going to say the same thing about *you,*" Gailyn remarked with a smile to the man.

He did look something like my father. When I shook his hand, though, it was large, hard, and crusted as earth. Whereas my father was a writer, this Saroyan was one of the tribe who had toiled with the earth, his skin sun-splashed, deep brown. It was good to see such a man coming to see my father, to know that my father's crops had mattered to him, as his own had mattered and given delight to my father.

We drove to my father's two houses, where the children picked some fruit from his trees, and Gailyn and I tried to get some sense of the interior of the houses, peering with difficulty through the cracks in the drawn shades. The rooms seemed to be sparsely furnished, though one we managed to see into, a sort of garagelike adjunct, was filled almost to the ceiling with cardboard boxes containing envelopes and magazines.

We had dinner at Balian's Armenian Restaurant in Fresno, and then drove home to Bolinas, arriving by midnight.

Last night at around six Ruben called to say that my father had told him that I was planning to come up and stay in his corner house, but that this was against the terms of the latest will, which he made out last September, and that according to those terms the house must remain sealed. I am not, therefore, to be given a key and allowed to use this house.

I might have suspected as much.

I had spent a great deal of time on the phone with Lucy yesterday, and Gailyn had talked with her a long time that morning, to lay the groundwork both practically and emotionally for a difficult, but we all felt worthwhile effort to see Pop through his final days, or weeks, or months.

We would set the place up so that we could all use it, perhaps eventually alternating visits, but beginning together, so that in the end Pop would be with his own family.

I visited the houses on both my visits to Fresno. They are essentially standard tract houses, but both have a variety of fruit trees—lemon, orange, apple, cherry, peach, and plum—in their front and back gardens. The kids might have enjoyed staying there off and on during the next weeks.

But, let me confess, I'm relieved. I knew yesterday that my visits with my father would be more and more difficult for me, that there would be no easy repetition of the trust and surrender of our first visit—that this, to all intents and purposes, had been a once-in-a-lifetime thing.

But I couldn't just let it go at that, at least not quite so simply, knowing he was still alive, without at least offering him our presence and care—not after what had happened between us.

Yet I could see on Sunday that it was going to be almost impossible for him to visit with us regularly without continuing his usual patterns of emotional grandstanding, and that in some essential way, this was to throw us all off the track: loud voice, funny remarks, but no real contact.

He is surrounded by the hospital staff and two cousins with whom he was never close, and I am quite certain now that this is the way he wants it.

The fact that he finds it impossible simply to say that this is the case, and ask me directly to go along with him, is some measure of the emotional contortion he must feel inside.

It is, also, for me, a deep regret and frustration. I will make sure Ruben's story is the truth—I will check on it through Dr. Aduan—but I don't really doubt it.

I have lived half of a full lifetime with these sad and maddening emotional impasses.

I will also ask Dr. Aduan to let my father know that if he should ever want to see me or my family, or Lucy, any or all of us, we will be happy to come up.

He is going now, passing out of this world, and I am going to let him go without further involvement. I'm tired of my own insistence, and his—however oblique, however ambivalent—resistance.

Let him go his way alone now, as he has always, essentially, preferred it. I am more grateful than I can say that at the very end of his life we shared a moment that I can remember and cherish unequivocally. I'm grateful, too, that he made up with Lucy, and saw Gailyn and his grandchildren one last time.

And what about the large truth in all of this that I remember speaking about at the beginning?

To me, it remains essentially the same sense of things I remember from the time I wrote that early entry.

Simply that we are, all of us, permeable membranes, capable of the most painful physical and psychic contortions, in need of wholehearted and full-bodied caring when we are children, and, if we don't get it, predictably and perhaps even inevitably, bound for trouble.

It may be an obvious thing to say, but perhaps it needs saying, just now, more than ever: children don't just grow up, they are "grown" up, the way a garden is grown.

My father was a one in a million accident, a child who emerged from a brutal, life-crushing childhood with a stamina and talent that had elements in it of genius. Nonetheless, in his deepest core, he remained twisted and tortured all his life.

It seems such a simple thing. If you keep a garden, you need sunlight, water, good soil, and the care of the gardener. If one or more of these essentials is missing, it will be difficult, if not impossible, to make it truly thrive, to make it truly beautiful.

In the end, in this way, I think each family is like a garden.

Last night, talking with Lucy on the phone several hours after I'd heard from Ruben—both of us now resigned to the fact that it was over, that we wouldn't be seeing Pop again—I read her the end of James Agee's review of the movie version of *The Time of Your Life*,

which appeared in *Time* of June 14, 1948—when I was
four, and she was two. This seems to me to be the most
clear-eyed and equitable assessment of my father, both
as an artist and—by extension—as a man, that I have
ever read. It is especially remarkable to me because
James Agee was one of my father's peers and contem-
poraries, and he wrote this review *at the time,* without
the advantage of the long view of his whole career. He
simply *saw:*

> Saroyan is an entertainer of a kind overrated by
> some people and underrated by others—a very gifted
> schmalz-artist. In the schmalz-artist strength and weak-
> ness are inextricably combined—the deeply, primor-
> dially valid, and the falseness of the middle-aged little
> boy who dives back into the womb for pennies.
>
> The schmalz-artist requires more belief, more wish-
> ful thinking on the part of his audience, than better
> artists would dare require. Reality is as much his
> deadly enemy as it is the superior artist's most difficult
> love affair. At his best, Saroyan is a wonderfully sweet-
> natured, witty and beguiling kind of Christian anar-
> chist, and so apt a lyrical magician that the magic
> designed for one medium still works in another. At his
> worst, he is one of the world's ranking contenders for
> brassy, self-pitying, arty mawkishness, for idealism
> with an eye to the main chance, for arrogant determi-
> nation to tell damnably silly lies in the teeth of the
> truth.
>
> Except in Saroyan's world, barroom philosophers
> who intrude on new customers with the words
> "What's the dream?" are seldom answered courte-
> ously; and when euphoria enchants any saloon for
> more than five consecutive minutes, you can expect a
> quick return of trouble, or boredom, or both. The face
> on Saroyan's barroom floor has something unassaila-
> bly good about the eyes. But the smile is that of a

swindling parson who is sure his own swindle is for the greater glory of God.

"That's incredible, Ar," Lucy said when I'd finished.

"And it was a really hard one to grow up with, Lu," I said. "Because he was really true and . . ."

"Really false," she said for me. "It was like when we were growing up, Ar, I used to apply his medicine for him for his athlete's foot, you know? I used to put it on his feet for him. And he would hold himself really rigid, and grit his teeth, and moan, and everything—I mean it was like it was practically killing him, you know?"

"Mmm-hmm."

"So, anyway," she continued, "you know that year I went to Northwestern—that year, somehow or other, *I* got athlete's foot. And so, I had to go and buy some of the medicine I used to put on Pop for him . . ."

"Un-hunh."

"So I got the medicine, and I went back to my room, really dreading having to put the medicine on, you know. I mean I knew it was going to really be horrible pain."

"Sure," I said.

"So, finally, I got myself together, you know, and I managed to put a little on—and, Ar, there was *no pain at all.* I mean *nothing.* It was completely *painless* medicine."

Although I didn't speak of it to Lucy on the phone, her story immediately reminded me of another incident with Pop one afternoon when he was visiting us at the house in Pacific Palisades.

I had done something that had made Lucy very angry at me, I think she may have even been crying, and she had asked Pop, or Papa, as we called him in those days, to give me a spanking, which my father, in fact, had never done with me.

My father, after a while, both agreed to do this and,

almost at the same time, managed to let me know that he wouldn't *really* spank me—not really hard, that is—and this way Lucy would be appeased, and I wouldn't really be hurt.

And so, after at first vehemently protesting, having been taken into his confidence in this way, I agreed to go through with it.

I must have been about nine at the time. I ended up willingly leaning across my father's lap to make it easy for him.

But when the spanking began, I found myself in the midst of a deep confusion, a deep ambivalence, that in its way might be considered a kind of small, but nevertheless exact, embodiment of the whole of my relationship with my father.

The spanking he gave me was real. It hurt. And yet, as I received it, I was torn between wanting to cry out in pain, and, at the same time, at an even deeper level, wanting the secret we'd shared, when he had taken me into his confidence to placate Lucy, to be real, to be a true communion between us. What did I do?

I went through the whole spanking pretending to myself that it didn't really hurt. Though I'm sure I made some sort of noise to satisfy Lucy, I never allowed the actual pain I was experiencing to become real to me. I steeled myself, to pretend that my father and I were actually friends.

And, at another level, I was genuinely confused about whether it actually did hurt. Perhaps I was being too weak to be hurt by what my father genuinely thought wasn't a real spanking.

This is it, then, in a nutshell. I am the son of a world-famous writer, a man people adore for his sweetness, but a man I know—in my deepest insides, where I knew that the spanking actually hurt—isn't the person people take him for. What do I do?

I do many things. I go up, and I go down. I become a writer—perhaps, among other reasons, to study my father even more intimately than I can in our actual life together. I get married and have children to explore at first hand the reality of a family, which eluded him and me as well in my own childhood. After years of marriage, after an auto accident, I end up, for the first time in my adult life, falling in love.

It is my wife I fall in love with, after all our years together. And now I see, at around the age my father was when he fell in love with my mother, just how powerful and unsettling it can be.

As we were driving toward the highway to Fresno on Sunday, still in the somewhat wooded area outside Samuel P. Taylor Park in Marin County, we had to slow our car along with others because there was a deer, a stag with horns—rare to see in these parts, though other deer are almost taken for granted—out in the middle of the road, and in a panic.

The stag was racing back and forth because one side of the road led down into civilization, a little roadside settlement, and the other side of the road, though promising a more wooded area, began with a sheer mountain cliff that went straight up at an almost 90-degree angle for a hundred feet or more before it leveled off.

Now as the deer raced from one side of the road to the other, trying to choose between two seeming impossibilities, more and more cars began converging on him, representing the most immediate threat of all, and one continuously increasing.

Suddenly the deer, by some amazing combination of panic and animal will, thrust himself up onto the sheer cliff, and by some miraculous force—stopping once to save himself when a foothold broke from under him—he scaled what was more in the nature of a wall than a mountain, all the way to the top.

The traffic had now halted on both sides in an area where, as I say, deer are taken for granted. What the stag had done, however, had been quite literally arresting, a feat that exceeded all expectation, that had seemingly defied fate itself.

As we drove on, there was for some time a hush among us all, even our three children.

"That deer was your father," Gailyn said a little farther down the road. "And what he did was your father's whole life."

For ten days or so after Ruben's call, I left my father alone, taking a breather and giving him the distance he seemed to want. Then, wondering what his condition might be now, I phoned the hospital and spoke with Dr. Aduan.

We had a long talk. His condition was worsening, but just how long he might go on, it would be hard for the doctor to say. He suggested that he ask my father, point blank, if he would like to have me visit him again, but I felt that this would be too direct. In the end, Dr. Aduan agreed to ask my father the more general question of whether he wished to see *anyone* whom he could get in touch with for him. He also would give him his own home phone number in case he wanted to contact him at a time when he wasn't at the hospital.

Apparently my father's mood had worsened; and he was now experiencing pain when he needed to move in bed as a nurse was attending him. I told Dr. Aduan that my sense was my father wanted to close down and go now, and that if this *was* the case, I didn't want to get in his way. The doctor said this was more or less the way he read the situation himself. Our talk, as I remember, was near the end of the week, probably on a Thursday.

On Saturday, I called the hospital and spoke with a nurse who was assigned to my father that day, and she told me that he had had a bloody stool, which was a sign that he could be nearing the end, though whether this was actually so, or just how long it might be, if it were so, was impossible for her to say.

The next day, Sunday, I made the decision to go down to Fresno and see him again, and to stay at a motel there and visit him daily for a while. I made arrangements to leave the following day. I was relieved to have finally come to a decision. I remember feeling unusually strong and clear that day.

On Monday morning, May 18, just after Gailyn had gotten up with the kids for school, there was a telephone call for me. I was still in bed, and though not asleep, not yet fully awake either. I got up and went to the phone in the living room. It was a cold, cloudy morning. A man identified himself to me as Dr. Macheski at the Veterans Administration Hospital in Fresno. He then told me that my father had passed away.

I hadn't heard him properly and I asked him to repeat it, which he did, apologizing for the abruptness of the call.

It was somehow hard for me to fathom, perhaps because I was just about to drive down to the hospital. After I got the specific time of my father's death, around seven that morning, just before the doctor had called me, I hung up the phone, walked into the center of the living room while at the same time telling Gailyn and the children the news, and then broke into tears, saying, "He was all alone. He died alone."

Quite by chance, over the weekend I'd come across an article in the newspaper about the misery of people who must die in institutions with no one by their side, and this had been a part of what had prompted my decision to go down to be with him again.

And now it was too late.

A short time later, I phoned my father's wing, Four East, at the hospital, and spoke with his night nurse, a

Mrs. Thornton, who was just going off duty. She told me that my father's niece, Jackie Kazarian, his sister Zabe's daughter, had been with him all night in his room.

This was like a blessing.

Later that morning I phoned Jackie at her home in Newport Beach. She had just arrived back on a flight from Fresno. I told her how grateful I was to her for being there, and how relieved, and she then told me about her time with Pop.

She had been talking with the night nurse every evening since hearing that my father had gone into the hospital and had suddenly had a strong impulse to see her Uncle Bill. Her own mother, Zabe, had also died of cancer and she had been with *her* on her last day, too, quite fortuitously, since she was the only one of four grown-up children who didn't live near her mother.

She'd arrived at the hospital the evening before, had gone to Pop's room, where he had apparently been restless and was having difficulty getting to sleep. She didn't seem certain that he recognized her, he seemed quite groggy, but with her arrival, he settled down almost immediately, and peacefully went to sleep.

She slept all night in a chair by his bed.

Then, early the next morning, just after she had woken up herself, he was suddenly awake and alert, and obviously recognized her and was happy to see her, although it was now impossible for him to speak.

She held his hand and spoke to him, telling him how much she loved him; and then she brought out a "Bless You" cookie, an American version of a Chinese fortune cookie, which she had brought with her for him. She opened it in front of him now, and read him his fortune: "Bless you with health and happiness."

He was obviously delighted she was there.

After a few more moments, she excused herself and said she was going to tell the nurse that he was up. He nodded, she left, and a few minutes later, she returned with the nurse. They found him asleep again now, and then, after examining him more closely, the night nurse realized with amazement that he had passed away.

Later in the day, I sent a telegram to the hospital, releasing my father's body into the custody of the Neptune Society, a next-of-kin formality.

By this time, the first news of his death had begun to break in the media, including the message he had left with the Associated Press—on the same call, apparently, during which he had revealed to them that he had cancer. The message, to be made public only after his death, was as follows: "Everybody has got to die, but I have always believed an exception would be made in my case. Now what?"

In the end, perhaps this statement capsulizes the enigma of my father's life better than anything more I might say. The strangest part, and for me the saddest, occurred to me a little while after I had heard this statement. I realized that probably the last genuinely intimate telephone conversation of his life had been with the Associated Press.

My father's will turned out much as I suspected it would. In fact, in a specific way which I have decided to leave out of this chronicle, it was quite a bit worse. He did make a provision for a small trust fund for Cosette, Lucy, me, and his three grandchildren, in the event that any of us should be in evident need, or in the event of an emergency. But this whole sum would be quickly exhausted if one of us needed serious and sustained medical care, for instance. On the other hand, this provision serves as a serious legal obstacle to contesting the will successfully—a course of action which promised, in any case, to be more expensive and time-consuming than it would be worth.

He left all of his personal possessions, all of his properties, all of his copyrights and future royalties, all of his published and unpublished manuscripts, all of his books and paintings and drawings, all of his correspondence and literary archives, and everything else that he owned, to the William Saroyan Foundation. In the end, he really had figured out a way to freeze his assets beyond death itself, and he carried it through. He created a foundation enshrining his own name, and this foundation will henceforth be funded and perpetuated by his estate. In effect, he left his estate to himself. He took it with him.

Ironically, my father himself summed the situation up for his hometown newspaper, the *Fresno Bee,* in the exclusive interview he gave them at his home on the day he signed his final will, April 11, 1981. Like his statement to the Associated Press, it was printed only after his death. His own words, which became the title of the newspaper article, were spoken with regard to how important the foundation was to him. But for me at least, they had an inescapable, if unwitting, second meaning. Under the smaller lead, "Saroyan's Will," the interview was headlined in large, boldfaced letters: " 'It's everything to me . . .' "